D1067545

MYTH PERFORMANCE IN THE AFRICAN DIASPORAS

Ritual, Theatre, and Dance

Benita Brown, Dannabang Kuwabong, and Christopher Olsen

THE SCARECROW PRESS, INC.
Lanham • Boulder • New York • Toronto • Plymouth, UK
2014

Published by Scarecrow Press, Inc.
A wholly owned subsidiary of Rowman & Littlefield
4501 Forbes Boulevard, Suite 200, Lanham, Maryland 20706
www.rowman.com

10 Thornbury Road, Plymouth PL6 7PP, United Kingdom

Copyright © 2014 by Scarecrow Press, Inc.

All rights reserved. No part of this book may be reproduced in any form or by any electronic or mechanical means, including information storage and retrieval systems, without written permission from the publisher, except by a reviewer who may quote passages in a review.

British Library Cataloguing in Publication Information Available

Library of Congress Cataloging-in-Publication Data

Brown, Benita, author.
Myth performance in the African diasporas : ritual, theatre, and dance / Benita Brown, Dannabang Kuwabong, and Christopher Olsen.
pages cm
Includes bibliographical references and index.
ISBN 978-0-8108-9279-8 (cloth : alk. paper) -- ISBN 978-0-8108-9280-4 (electronic)
1. Drama—Black authors—History and criticism. 2. Mythology, African, in literature. 3. English literature—African influences. 4. Dance, Black—History and criticism. 5. Africa—Influence.
I. Kuwabong, Dannabang, 1955– II. Olsen, Christopher, 1952– III. Title.
PN1590.B53B76 2014
812.0080896—dc23
2013034434

♾ ™The paper used in this publication meets the minimum requirements of American National Standard for Information Sciences Permanence of Paper for Printed Library Materials, ANSI/NISO Z39.48-1992.

Printed in the United States of America

CONTENTS

ACKNOWLEDGMENTS

We wish to acknowledge the following people and entities whose invaluable help has made the writing of this book possible. First, we give thanks to the African deities and historical figures whose spiritual presence guided us throughout the writing of this book. Second, we give thanks to the ancestors of the African Diaspora whose vision, spirit, courage, tenacity, and faith throughout their struggle to maintain their humanity gave us hope that this project could be achieved. Third, we give thanks to the living descendants of the African Diaspora described in this study that keep on translating and keeping the faith in the myths and vision of their fore-parents in drama and dance. Fourth, this work would not have been possible without the financial support of, first, Virginia State University and, subsequently, an Institutional Research Fund / Fondo Institucional para la Investigación (FIPI) grant from the Decanato de Estudios Graduados e Investigación (DEGI), University of Puerto Rico, Rio Piedras. Fifth, we could not have completed this work without the help of, first, Javier Cruz, who worked as the first research assistant under the FIPI grant, and, second, Keila Alemán, who has worked tirelessly in the past year to put the final draft of the manuscript in order. We also wish to acknowledge Professor Reinhard Sander of the University of Puerto Rico who gave freely of his time to read over drafts of some chapters and offered invaluable advice. Recognition must also be given to all the performers who have graciously given us permission to use photographs of their work to enhance the book's presentation. Finally, we wish to thank all those who in one way or another helped to make the writing of this book possible but whose names are too numerous to list here.

INTRODUCTION

Ritual Journeys, Dancing Histories,
Enacting Bodies, and Spirits

Dannabang Kuwabong

The idea of writing a book that examines the concept and practice of myth performance in African Diaspora dramas and dances originated during a discussion among three of us—Dr. Benita Brown, professor in African dance and performance at Virginia State University; Dr. Christopher Olsen, professor of drama in the English department, University of Puerto Rico, Rio Piedras Campus, San Juan; and me, Dr. Dannabang Kuwabong, professor of Caribbean literature in the Department of English, University of Puerto Rico, Rio Piedras Campus, San Juan—at the National Association of African American Studies and Affiliates Conference held in Baton Rouge, Louisiana, in February 2008. This idea was born out of the realization that our conference presentations all dealt with aspects of how myth, legend, history, and performance as themes in African Diaspora drama and dance have not been dealt with in any substantial and integrated manner. August Wilson's (493–503) words ground and validate our idea that through drama and dance performance, Africans in Diaspora have created new mythopoeic narratives and developed indestructible performance praxes that affirm their Afrisporic[1] worldview. In these praxes, recuperative historicity is engaged to invoke, evoke, and mythicize historical Africans of the past as agents to help them confront the contradictory presents and uncertainties about their own cultural and historical location and their full participation in a Europhonic dominated historiography of the Americas.

African Diaspora cultural producers and intellectual activists have, since the 1800s, developed discursive maneuvers in drama and dance to re-configure and re-establish great African historical figures and deities, as well as the not-so-well-known individuals whose bodies became *cartes blanches* on which Europeans projected their visions of Africa. Our purpose in this collection of six essays is to join in this discursive praxis, not to regurgitate representational ideas of Atlantic African Diasporas, but to celebrate, as August Wilson has observed, African American (United States, Canada, Latin America) and African Caribbean peoples' demonstrated abilities to create, recreate, maintain, and perform their connectivity with both their immediate and distant worlds through dramatic (re)mythicization of historical Africans celebrated in the dual histories of the Western European and Arab worlds. Articulating their historical connectivity helps to establish a continuous, not necessarily linear, trend between the various brands of African Diaspora experiences and struggles.

The plays and performances we have explored in these essays testify to their hitherto unstudied performative evocations and invocations of Africa's sons and daughters, both in Diaspora and in their colonized African locales (Roman times), and how they echo but, nonetheless, predate a poignant keynote address delivered by the late president and father of modern-day Guinea, Ahmed Sekou Toure. At the Second Congress of Black Writers and Artists held in Rome in 1959, well attended by several African American pioneers of the Harlem Renaissance and also Caribbean writers of the Negritude movement, Sekou Toure's call for revolutionary praxes among African and African Diaspora writers still resonates with urgency today:

> To take part in the African revolution it is not enough to write a revolutionary song, you must fashion the revolution with the people. And if you fashion it with the people, the songs will come by themselves, and of themselves. In order to achieve real action, you must yourself be a living part of Africa and of her thought; you must be an element of that popular energy which is entirely called forth for the freeing, the progress, and the happiness of Africa. There is no place outside that fight for the artist or for the intellectual who is concerned

with and completely at one with the people in the great battle of Africa
and of suffering humanity. (qtd. in Fanon 206)

Even though Sekou Toure was addressing his concerns primarily to
continental African writers and artists, his words were and are, nevertheless, pertinent to any project of cultural, racial, and historical recuperation
among any peoples of African descent. In spite of the fact that the situations confronting each group may be slightly different, as agued by the
African Americans at the conference (Jules-Rosette 49–83), there are
historical experiences, often mythical and of epic dimensions, that connect them all. For that reason, it is important to examine the narrative and
performance elements of epic and myth in the plays by Africans in Diaspora. In the present work, the three authors examine various dramatic
texts and dance performances within the grand design of African Diaspora peoples' search for cultural liberation. Through the selected scribal and
dance performance texts, the authors give broader interpretations of how
African Diaspora communities have managed to secure their cultural futures. This work then is an extension of individual but brief and scattered
studies that recognize African Diaspora drama and dance performances as
playing pivotal socially committed roles in tapping into the mythic world
of African cultures and the creative forces that have ensured the survival
of people of African Diaspora (Ayejina 397–404; Wilson-Tagoe 169–81).

This social commitment is tied to the type of theatrical performance
dramatists of the African Diaspora have created from remembered festival theatres in which ethnic histories, myths, and legends are often performed through dances, drama, and ritual, together with symbiotic adaptations of new-world realities of European languages and cultural paradigms.

Recognizing, therefore, that performance studies across many disci-
plines have become major areas of academic research in the past twenty
years, the authors of the six chapters in the book successfully yoke together different essays that reflect an interdisciplinary approach in con-
tent and interpretation to myth performance in drama and dance. Similarly, research in postcolonialism, gender/sexuality, intercultural studies,
and literary studies, among others, vigorously engages and features core
components of performance and myth in articulating interpretative strategies. This sharing of similar components demonstrates the interrelated-
ness of these fields of knowledge. Thus, although African Diaspora stud-

ies continue to expand in range and scope, there still remains fertile terrain for investigating multiple techniques of myth, creation, and interpretation through dance performance, history as performance, dramatic narrative, and staged rituals. This book is hence designed to expand the study of African Diaspora cultural studies from this angle.

In addition, because history, spirituality, and cultural formation strategies often overlap with myth, the positions taken by the three authors on myth performance in drama and dance rituals are not limited to one interpretive dimension; rather, the authors take a multiplicity of positions in which myths are read as entailing multiple narratives of origin. The authors' definitions of myth reject any limited theories of ontological monogenesis. Thus, for example, the chapters on how Africans in Diaspora perform dance rituals either in secular drama or sacred worship spaces to celebrate African deities do not focus on purity of forms or history per se, but how these are re-enacted in the new environments to suit new realities. The authors examine how historical figures are reconfigured and re-presented on stage as mythical/legendary role models for the African Diaspora societies. Subsequently, the authors look at myth performance and dance as African Diaspora cultural cognitive lodestars (touchstones) that give African Diaspora peoples new orientations and visions, liberation of spirit, and a cultural clearing and bearing within what seem to be otherwise chaotic and stifling environments.

The authors read myths as performative transformations of depositories of accumulated practical wisdom of Africans in the African continent and in Diaspora. They identify these transformations in myth performances and dances as processes of intuitive symbolization and as constructive new realities in new and sacred rituals or staged secular performances. Myths in these contexts, as posited by the authors, are neither true nor false narratives, but new revelations of the inner relationships of African Diaspora peoples with their non-African environments. They are constructive, adaptive strategies and responses originating in dynamic intergenerational observations and experiences to structure a meaning to their existence. Subsequently, African Diaspora myths, performances, and dances seek and (re)create psychosocial, psychosomatic, cultural, historical, spiritual, and emotional orientations, bearings, and stabilizations.

Therefore, the three authors claim that their book fulfills a great and urgent need to explore African-derived myths and performances in the

new cultural landscapes to which African peoples were dispersed, and
they do so through their new strategy of reading new African Diaspora
cultural productions within a global context. Thus, the six chapters in the
book reveal a connectedness of various artistic elements, elements that
unify these cultural productions, especially in the fields of drama and
dance. In chapter 1, Kuwabong explores the multiple perspectives needed
to read these cultural productions. His chapter establishes the definitions
underlining the historical, cultural, and literary frameworks, and it foregrounds the intellectual arguments of the succeeding chapters. His chapter reveals the ways historical African figures in the Arab and Asiatic
worlds are performed in plays of Willis Richardson, Maud Cuney-Hare,
Derek Walcott, and Aimé Césaire as countercultural histories necessary
for the development of new historical and cultural imaginaries by African
Diaspora peoples. In the process, he demonstrates how these writers manage to create new mythologies from ancient African histories, which then
function as lodestars of racial pride for African Americans and African
Caribbean peoples. The engagement of performance/dramaturgic elements by these writers—dance, song, poetry, ritual, and masquerade—
enhance the central themes of the dramas and act to elevate the central
characters to the level of culture heroes. As a corollary to Kuwabong's
position, and as a further extension of the role of dance and ritual performances in African Diaspora communities, Brown brilliantly gives com-
pelling arguments for the exploration of the multiple dance movements,
music, and other performance techniques in African Diaspora communities that create ritual spaces for the entry of the African deities. Kuwabong's historical and secular perspectives prepare the clearing for
Brown's more religious focus on the sacred aspects of African ritual
dances as myth performance. Olsen's chapter then focuses on the colonized Black female body, symbolic of the African continent, as an object
of European curiosity and construction of hierarchized differences and
negative othering. He reads Parks's *Venus* as a re-examination of the life
of Sara Baartman, a Khoikhoi/Xhoza woman, who had been kidnapped
and brought to Europe during the Victorian era, renamed Venus Hottentot, and displayed as an antithesis to Venus, the paragon of European
female sexuality. Olsen shows how Parks rewrites Sara Baartman's history and, in the process, gives her voice and agency. He argues that the play
is Parks's counter-poetic that contests the negative stereotypes and myths

of the Black female body that still pervade the epistemology of Euro-American sexual politics of race and gender.

As a unique approach to the understanding of myth performance and dance in African Diaspora, these six essays, discordant in style and presentation as they may seem, nonetheless chart a new path that ultimately enriches and further enhances the understanding of African Diaspora myth performance in literary and diaspora studies. Wole Soyinka's *Myth, Literature and the African World*; *Black Theatre: Ritual Performance in the African Diaspora*, edited by Paul Carter Harrison, Victor Leo Walker Jr., and Gus Edwards; Paul Carter Harrison's *The Drama of Nommo*; and Errol Hill's edited collection of essays, *The Theatre of Black Americans*, all contain aspects of what our book is about. But while Soyinka's text is limited to the Yoruba worldview and hence is criticized for being Yoruba-centric, the later texts are collections of formerly published essays and do not deal with contemporary drama or performances. In addition, none of these deal with the issues of myth performance and dance in the African Diaspora from a global perspective.

This book is also about archival retrieval of otherwise silenced voices. Cultures emerging among African Diaspora populations in Caribbean, North American, Latin American, and European multicultural centers have developed new interpretations of African-derived myths to reflect their own particularities. The authors hope that their unique approach to this topic—bringing together research in theatre, dance, and literary "texts"—will chart another path in the global exploration of African Diaspora myth making, mythologizing, and performance through dance and drama. Myth making means the creation of a new myth from an original myth while mythologizing implies a reinterpretation of a historical narrative, an existing myth, a legend, with the intent of redefining it to suit new social parameters.

A brief summary of each chapter as they are arranged in the book is in order at this point. In chapter 1, "Re-visionary History as Myth Performance: A Postcolonial Re-reading of Maud Cuney-Hare's *Antar of Araby*, Willis Richardson's *The Black Horseman*, and Aimé Césaire's *And the Dogs Were Silent*," Kuwabong explores how Willis Richardson's *The Black Horseman* and Maud Cuney-Hare's *Antar of Araby* draw inspiration from Pharaonic, Carthaginian, and pre-Islamic worlds to craft dramas of radical departures that contribute to the reactive project of cultural substitution toward the nurturing of "authentic" African Diaspora voices

in the artificially racialized spaces in the United States' cultural, historical, and educational industries. His approach to these plays from a problematic postcolonial critical location signals his understanding of the ideological parallels that underpin the cultural, historical, and political strategies engaged by African Americans, Afro-Caribbean people, and continental Africans to liberate their people from Eurocentric ideological and/
or political colonialism. Thus, though the plays are remarkably different
in styles and historical locations, they nonetheless employ similar performance elements that border on the ritualistic and heroic. This chapter sets
out to demonstrate how the playwrights use drama to articulate their
various positions on the recall of their African cultural, political, and
spiritual heritages. It opens up the various arguments that are engaged by
all three authors in their essays and gives credence to the position taken
by the authors that African Diaspora myth performances in drama and
dance across geographic and historical locations are interlinked by ideological underpinnings and cultural art forms.

In chapter 2, "The Òrìṣà Paradigm: An Overview of African-Derived
Mythology, Folklore, and Kinesthetic Dance Performatives," Brown
makes a strong case for reconsideration of the sacred rituals and the
celebrations of West African (Yoruba) deities and heroes by Africans
brought to the Americas through dance and music. She asserts that though
initially these cultural performances from West Africa were temporarily
displaced by Christianity, European cultures, societal acceptance, and
political and paralegal infringements during slavery and post-emancipa-
tion, they were not completely erased from the cell memories of Africans
in these new locations. This, she argues, is testified to by the Harlem
Renaissance, which documents an African-based cultural revolution
among African Americans during the early 1900s to 1940s. She argues
further that this cultural phenomenon was not isolated in time and space:
grassroots, cultural experiences in dance, music, drama, literature, art,
and the oral tradition had been preserved as a consistent reminder of their
African roots among Africans in the Americas. Thus, Brown uses this
position to focus on the latent spiritual experiences present in grassroots
dance forms (accompanied by its music) that occurred in the North Philadelphia community (as in many other communities throughout the
African Diaspora). These cultural practices, she contends, though originally full of ritual texts and subtexts, lost over time their purposeful
reenactment of religious mythology. Nonetheless, she maintains that

these same dance forms and music, with their secular overtones, still maintain at some subliminal level a collective unconscious that reveals undercurrents of the sacred insofar as West African–derived consciousness of time and space, food, material culture, music, and the oral tradition are concerned.

Olsen in chapter 3, "Performative Body Language in Suzan-Lori Parks's *Venus* and Lynn Nottage's *Ruined*: African Female Bodies through African-American Eyes," engages the reader in a close reading of how African women, or for that matter Black female bodies, have been recuperated from sexualized othering for the scrutinizing and negative gaze of the European male and turned into symbolic tropes of courage and fortitude. He maintains that, through these dramas, the ideology of victimhood that has operated in the writings of most African Diaspora females becomes a launchpad for a new type of empowering epistemology, a new voice and agency, that elevates the one who had been a victim to a position of victory over oppression. The fact that centuries of sexploitation and racism have not succeeded in vanquishing the tenacity of spirit of African Diaspora women is a testimonial to their spirit of survival. Olsen then suggests that both playwrights manipulate the semiotic nature of the vivid image of an African woman's body on stage in order to expose these bodies as shock therapy against the hierarchical phallocentric gaze of the reader/audience and as a device to embolden and empower African Diaspora females. Olsen goes on to insist that both Parks and Nottage, by their exploration of African/Black female bodies in their work, here not only succeed in demystifying old mythologies constructed about these bodies but, in the process, create new contestatory and proactive mythologies through African storytelling techniques. Olsen even goes further to show how, in 2008, Nottage's *Ruined* is culturally authenticated through its use of actual interviews of Congolese women who survived the violence and destruction of two civil wars, thus linking the present ravages visited on the African women's bodies today with what European colonial brigandage had done in the nineteenth century.

Benita Brown's "The Codification of Soul in African-Derived Dance Culture" is a descriptive analysis of the appearance of West African deities in North America during ritual ceremonies (called Bembe') among African Americans. She describes how ritual ecstatic dances emanate from Yoruba myths about their deities and discusses the behavioral characteristics of these deities as enacted in dance, music, song, and drama.

Brown focuses on Yoruba because that seems to be the most visible West African group in the Americas whose rituals are well established and studied in the new world. Of course, she is not arguing here that only the Yoruba traditions are present among the African Diaspora communities, as one is never sure of any purity of cultural retentions and there are so many similarities among African traditions. Brown is therefore aware that other West and Central African cultures must have been appropriated into what is now known as the Òrìṣà in the new world. Also, the Yoruba were among the last large importation of Africans to arrive in the new world at the very end of the slave trade and were thus able to keep a greater portion of their religious rites and cultural norms under the guise of Catholic Christianity. They disguised their own myth narratives, rituals, performances, dances, and music at the grassroots level. Through the allegories of dance, music, song, and drama, Africans communicated, adhered to, invoked, appeased, and conferred thanks for blessings received from the Almighty God through divine deities emanating from creolized and syncretic Yoruba spiritual practices. Devotees were able to pray specifically for blessings of health, love, money, and general well-being while appealing to their deities' particular characteristics and attributes within a outwardly Catholic Christian tradition.

Following Brown's argument that Yoruba traditions were disguised and performed under Western eyes, in chapter 5, "Of Rebels, Tricksters, and Supernatural Beings: Toward a Semiotics of Myth Performance in African Caribbean and Afro-Brazilian Dramas," Kuwabong engages multiple evaluative processes to uncover and explain the plethora of recurrent tropes and cultural signs and symbols manifested in African Caribbean and Afro-Brazilian dramas. The texts used for his critical reading—a shift from Brown's descriptive analysis—are Carril's *Shango de Irma*; Nascimento's *Sortilege II: Zumbi Returns*; and Gilkes's *Couvade: A Dream Play of Guyana*. In his analysis, Kuwabong addresses African Diaspora dramatic re-creation of West African religious rituals and myth performances that draws on a repertoire of re-membered historical, cultural, and supernatural tropes and figures, and presents them on stage in order to construct tentative cohesions of collective consciousness. He argues that the plays are pivotal to a program of resurrecting, renaming, rezoning, reactivating, and institutionalizing ancient African religious myths in their new locations, thus contextualizing the deep-rooted desires of African Diaspora peoples for a sense of historical and cultural person-

hood and belongingness, and possibly for psychic returns to the motherland, Africa. But these dramas also present arguments for the rootedness
of these African-generated performances, a rootedness that encapsulates
other traditions with which the African came into contact, including the
traditions of the indigenous peoples of the Guyana hinterland; the Tainos,
Arawaks, and Caribs of the Caribbean; and the Native peoples of Brazil,
mixed with Asian and European cultures. Thus, Kuwabong draws on
histories of migrations, resistance to slavery and cultural indoctrination,
and the role of artists and writers in the project of liberation. The plays, he
argues, do not proselytize a return to Africa in a romanticized form, but a
return to African-derived roots in the new world without preaching a
message of cultural purity or exclusivity. Thus, the new myth of a return
to Africa is questioned as the plays seem to say Africa is right here in the
Diaspora.

It is this questioning of an earlier return to a mythic Africa that Olsen's essay, "Of Princesses and Queens: The Mythical Journeys Home in
Djanet Sears's *Afrika, Solo* and Rebecca Fisseha's *Wise.Woman*," pro-
blematizes as a fitting end to the book. As Olsen shows, these plays
reveal the unseen problems in making a physical journey back to a romanticized and/or imaginary African homeland, a distant exotic place
now perceived through mythical lenses where reality is filtered through
wishful desires. Olsen contends that when describing the relationship
between one's place in the Diaspora and this imagined homeland as the
place of one's self-completion, without taking into account the centuries
of cultural creolization that have taken place both in the Diaspora and in
the "homeland," "black diasporic pilgrims" often "unadvisedly" insert
themselves into an African setting focusing solely on their metaphysical
and spiritual changes but losing a sense of the African context. Thus, to
such pilgrims, Africa becomes a fossilized symbolic object to be repos-
sessed by her erstwhile "lost" children. It is this problematic relationship
between Diaspora Africans and Africans on the continent that Djanet
Sears, an African Canadian playwright, dramatizes in *Afrika, Solo* (1987).
Here, the protagonist undertakes the physical journey back to Africa in
which she acts as a storyteller and performance artist on stage and re-
enacts her experiences as she travels throughout the continent. Olsen sees
a link between this play and *Wise.Woman* (2009) by Rebecca Fisseha, an
Ethiopian Canadian. Fisseha's play is not about a search for roots but
rather a conflicted response to a return to Africa to get married—an act

itself symbolic of reconnecting with Africa—so that she never loses her roots but passes them on to her children. Thus both plays, contends Olsen, are journeys of self-discovery, cultural education, de-mystification, and de-mythologizing—what Zara Bennett called "The Foiled Myth of Return." Of course, Ama Ata Aidoo had in 1964 taken this issue up in her classic play, *The Dilemma of a Ghost.*

Finally, as this collection of essays shows, there is a lot more yet to be done, especially in the area of comparative studies in myth performance in drama and dance, not only between the African Diaspora and Africa, but also among African Diaspora cultures. The differences and similarities between various Caribbean islands, Latin and Central American nations, North American countries, and European nations where there are large populations of African Diaspora peoples must be studied to fully grasp the global nature and significance of these ongoing cultural praxes. There is the need to study how African Caribbean people have rearticulated their Africanness within a Caribbeanness while relocated in the new empires such as the United States, Canada, and Europe, and to see how these contest for or add to the space already created in the plays we have examined.

NOTE

1. I coin and use the term "Afrisporic" as a word that connotes and denotes a neuter gender. It is a combination of Africa and Diasporic. The other terms, "Afrosporic" and "Afrasporic," retain an essentialism that perpetuates gender wars between people of African descent in their dialogues of representation of their African Diaspora personhoods.

WORKS CITED

Aidoo, Ama Ata. "The Dilemma of a Ghost." *The Dilemma of a Ghost and Anowa.* London: Longman, 1995. Print.

Ayejina, Funso. "The Death and Rebirth of African Deities in Edward Kamau Braithwaite's *Islands*." *WLWE* 23.2 (1984): 397–404. Print.

Bennett, Zara. "Going Home? The Foiled Myth of Return in Eddy L. Harris's *Native Stranger: A Black American's Journey into the Heart of Africa* and Caryl Phillip's *The Atlantic Sound.*" *Paroles gelées* 22.1 (2006): 7–17. Print.

Carril, Pepe. *Shango de Irma: A Yoruba Mystery Play.* English adaptation with a preface by Susan Sherman. Introduction by Jerome Rethenberg and Edward James. Garden City, NY: Doubleday, 1969, 1970. Print.

Césaire, Aimé. *And the Dogs Were Silent. Lyric and Dramatic Poetry 1946–82*. Trans. Clayton Eshleman and Annette Smith. Charlottesville: UP of Virginia, 1996, 1999. 3–74. Print.

Cuney-Hare, Maud. *Antar of Araby. Plays and Pageants from the Life of the Negro*. Ed. Willis Richardson. Jackson: UP of Mississippi, 1993. Print.

Fanon, Franz. *The Wretched of the Earth*. Trans. Constance Farrington. New York: Grove, 1959. Print.

Fisseha, Rebecca. *Wise.Woman*. Unpublished Manuscript, 2009. Print.

Gilkes, Michael. *Couvade: A Dream-Play of Guyana*. London: Dongaroo, 1988. Print.

Harrison, Paul Carter, Victor Leo Walker II, and Gus Edwards, eds. *Black Theatre: Ritual Performance in the African Diaspora*. Philadelphia: Temple UP, 2002. Print.

Jules-Rosette, Bennetta. *Black Paris: The African Writers' Landscape*. Foreword by Simon Njami. Chicago: U of Illinois P, 1988. Print.

Nascimento, Abdias do. *Sortilege II: Zumbi Returns*. Trans. with introduction by Elisa Larkin Nascimento. *Crosswinds: An Anthology of Black Dramatists in the Diaspora*. Ed. with introduction by William B. Branch. Bloomington: Indiana UP, 1993. 203–49. Print.

Nottage, Lynn. *Ruined*. Manhattan Theatre Club Production, directed by Kate Whoriskey. Playscript draft. February 4, 2009. Print.

Parks, Suzan-Lori. *The American Play and Other Works*. New York: Theatre Communications Group, 1995. Print.

Richardson, Willis, ed. *Plays and Pageants from the Life of the Negro*. Jackson: UP of Mississippi, 1993. Print.

Sears, Djanet. *Afrika, Solo* in *Afrika Solo, Come Good Rain, Je me souviens*. Ed. Ric Knowles. Toronto: Playwrights Canada Press, 2011. Print.

Soyinka, Wole. *Myth, Literature, and the African World*. Cambridge: Cambridge UP. 1976. Print.

Toure, Sekou Ahmed. Keynote address to the Congress of Black Writers and Artists held in Rome in 1959. Cited in Franz Fanon, *The Wretched of the Earth*. Trans. Constance Farrington. New York: Grove, 1959. Print.

Wilson, August. "The Ground on which I Stand." *Callaloo* 20.3 (1998): 493–503. Print.

Wilson-Tagoe, Nana. "From Myth to Dialectic: History in Derek Walcott's Drama." *Historical Thought in West Indian Literature*. Miami: UP of Florida, 1998. 169–81. Print.

I

RE-VISIONARY HISTORY AS MYTH PERFORMANCE

A Postcolonial Re-reading of Maud Cuney-Hare's *Antar of Araby*, Willis Richardson's *The Black Horseman*, and Aimé Césaire's *And the Dogs Were Silent*

Dannabang Kuwabong

African diasporic historical dramas such as Maud Cuney-Hare's *Antar of Araby*, Willis Richardson's *The Black Horseman*, Aimé Césaire's *And The Dogs Were Silent*, *The Tragedy of Henry Christophe*, and *A Season in the Congo*, Djanet Sears's *Angelique*, and Derek Walcott's *Henry Christophe*, *Dream on Monkey Mountain*, among others, can be read as postcolonial revisionary historical dramas using patterns delineated by Shelby Steele in "Notes on Ritual in New Black Theatre," Eleanor W. Taylor's "Two Afro-American Contributions to Dramatic Forms," Kimberley W. Benston's "The Aesthetic of Modern Black Drama: From Mimesis to Methexis," William Cook's "Mom, Dada, and God: Values in Black Theatre," and Larry Neale's "Into Nationalism, Out of Parochialism," among others. I am aware of the problematic position I enter in this claim, considering the debates about what it means to be defined as a colonized people that raged between African American authors and Afro-Caribbean and African writers at the dawn of the Negritude movement in Paris of the 1950s. Nonetheless, I use the term *postcolonial* then to signal my understanding of the ideological parallels that underpinned the cultural, historical, and political strategies engaged by African Americans,

Afro-Caribbean people, and continental Africans to liberate their people from Eurocentric ideological and political colonialism. The plays enact rituals of race memories through performance. In these rituals, reality is mythicized and enters into the realm of cultural histories.

Likewise, Paul Carter Harrison in *The Drama of Nommo* argues that African Diaspora theatrical performance is "imbued in the life experience [as] race memory" (194). He echoes Alain Locke's prescription that the "finest function [of] . . . race drama would be to supply an imaginative channel of escape and spiritual release, and by some process of emotional reinforcement to cover life with the illusion of . . . spiritual freedom" (iv). Harrison furthers this position by stressing that "the aims of the black theater are inspired by a social ethic which is diametrically opposed to the presumed cultural hierarchy of the Western world" (195). Consequently, the dramatic re-presentation of historical African or African Diaspora themes, heroes, and heroines through pageants translates into praxes of mythicization. As stated in the introduction, mythicization in this case is a dehistoricized and reconfigured exhibition of African historical themes to create imaginary spaces for the superimposition of African Diaspora real-ities. Through acts of superimposition, African Diaspora playwrights dis-turb and destabilize Eurocentric narratives, couched as history that oc-cludes African contributions to world civilizations. Maud Cuney-Hare, Willis Richardson, Aimé Césaire, and Derek Walcott, among others, en-gage their diasporic imaginaries and rhetorics of retrievals to enact narra-tives of performance that seek to erase any inner contradictions about Africa whose historical figures they appropriate to re-define and re-vision their own struggles and projected achievements.

Subsequently, in *The Black Horseman* (179–218), Richardson uses Bosioba and Casintha as race signifiers to problematize African Diaspora identity polemics, which Franz Fanon, Kathy Russell et al., Kimberle Williams Crenshaw, Hortense Spillers, Margaret Hunter, and Margo Nat-alie Crawford, among others, have argued engage acts of simplification to dilute the anxieties of colorism that are daily played out in African Di-asporic interracial, intraracial, and gender relations. As a result, rather than battle with the epidermal complexities and heterogeneity he finds in Africa, Richardson chooses to superimpose the racialized politics of the United States of America on historical African politics of geography and class. In so doing, Richardson visualizes an Africa through racialized lenses in which the darker-complexioned African is set up as normative to combat white racism. This kind of racialized radicalization of Afrocentricity, argues A. B. Spellman in his critique of the Black Arts movement of the 1960s in "Big Bushy Afros," fails to fully incorporate and utilize the complicated and rich diversity of races, colors, kinships, languages, cultures, and beliefs that undermine the African Diaspora nationalist discourse. In other words, the setting up of black pigmentocracy as resistance to white Eurocentricity becomes a narrow nationalism that engages the dangerous rhetoric of racial essentialism. For instance, in essentializing Sophonisba, Bosioba, and Casintha, he reinstates the darker-pigmented Black woman in a slippery category of normative purity into which lighter-skinned African Americans must then strive to enter.

Notwithstanding the dangers of this kind of politics, essentialization was perhaps a necessary tool at this point to establish a somatic historicity in which pigmentocracy becomes a trajectory from which to project African Diasporic narratives of historical retrieval. Moreover, Richardson does not engage this position in a historical and geographic void, but starts from the historical life-and-death struggles between Europe (Roman Empire) and Africa (Numidia), often called the Punic Wars. By using this period as a historical backdrop, Richardson traverses the Atlantic and the Mediterranean, while maintaining a political foothold in the Americas—a dream move that validates what August Wilson (493–593) testifies to as hallowed foundations that African diasporic dramatists and performers build on:

I have come here today to make a testimony, to talk about the ground on which I stand and all the many grounds on which I and my ancestors have toiled, and the ground of theater on which my fellow artists and I have labored to bring forth its fruits, its daring and its sometimes lacerating, and often healing, truths. An important part of Black Theater that is often ignored but is seminal to its tradition is its origins on the slave plantations of the South. Summoned to the big house to entertain the slave owner and his guests, the slave began a tradition of theater as entertainment for whites that reached its pinnacle in the heyday of the Harlem Renaissance. This entertainment for whites consisted of whatever the slave imagined or knew that his master wanted to see and hear. This tradition has its present life counterpart in the crossover artists that slant their material for white consumption:

> I stand myself and my art squarely on the self-defining ground of
> the slave quarters and find the ground to be hallowed and made
> fertile by the blood and bones of the men and women who can be
> described as warriors on the cultural battlefield that affirmed their
> self-worth. As there is no idea that cannot be contained by Black
> life, these men and women found themselves to be sufficient and
> secure in their art and their instructions. (493–94)

Wilson's words show that Africans in Diaspora have developed indestructible performance praxes that perpetuate an affirmation of their personhoods. In these praxes, recuperative historicity is engaged to invoke,
evoke, and ritualize through performance historical Africans, who then
help them to confront contemporary contradictions and uncertainties
about their own cultural, racial, and historical location and full participation in the Americas. Subsequently, African diasporic cultural producers
and intellectual activists from the 1800s onward sought to develop discursive maneuvers to re-establish great Africans of the past as signifiers of
their own present-day struggles.

I join in this discursive praxis not to regurgitate representational ideas
of Atlantic African Diasporas but to celebrate, as August Wilson has
observed, African American and African Caribbean peoples' demonstrated abilities to create, recreate, maintain, and perform their connectivity
with both their immediate and distant worlds through dramatic
(re)mythicization of historical Africans celebrated in the dual histories of
the Western European and Arab worlds. The importance of articulating
African diasporic historical connectivity is seen in how that helps to
establish a continuous, not necessarily linear, trend between the various
brands of African Diaspora experiences and struggles. The plays I explore here therefore for their performative evocation and invocation of
Africa's sons and daughters, both in Diaspora and in their colonized
locales (Roman times), echo but nonetheless predate a poignant keynote
address delivered by Ahmed Sekou Toure at the Second Congress of
Black Writers and Artists held in Rome in 1959. This congress was well
attended by several African American pioneers of the Harlem Renaissance and also Caribbean writers of the Negritude movement. Sekou
Toure's call for revolutionary praxes among African and African Diaspora writers still resonates with urgency today:

To take part in the African revolution it is not enough to write a revolutionary song, you must fashion the revolution with the people. And if you fashion it with the people, the songs will come by themselves, and of themselves.

In order to achieve real action, you must yourself be a living part of Africa and of her thought; you must be an element of that popular energy which is entirely called forth for the freeing, the progress, and the happiness of Africa. There is no place outside that fight for the artist or for the intellectual who is concerned with and completely at one with the people in the great battle of Africa and of suffering humanity. (qtd. in Fanon 206)

Even though Sekou Toure was addressing his concerns primarily to continental African writers and artists, his words were and are, nevertheless, pertinent to any project of cultural, racial, and historical recuperation among all peoples of African descent. In spite of the fact that the situations confronting each group may be slightly different, as the African Americans at the conference argued (49–83), there are historical experiences, often mythical and of epic dimensions, that connect them all. For that reason, it is important to examine the narrative and performance elements of epic and myth in the plays by Africans in Diaspora. In this chapter, I read three plays by African Americans in due recognition of their intended role in the grand design of the African American search for a drama of cultural liberation through historical revisionism. In another chapter, I discuss the drama of the Caribbean within the context of the pivotal role in myth making as a creative force that ensures the survival of people of African Caribbean descent.

Franz Fanon in *The Wretched of the Earth* complicates the ideological positioning of Sekou Toure by expanding its implications. In order to fulfill Toure's call to action by writers and artists toward the liberation of people of African descent, he argues that, for African peoples in the colonized societies of Africa, the Caribbean, and without doubt the United States, each generation and community of African people, be they on the continent of Africa or in Diaspora, must "discover its own mission or betray it" (Fanon 206–7). Those of us born in these times, Fanon asserts then, must embrace the historic mission, which "is to sanction all revolts, all desperate actions, all those abortive attempts drowned in the rivers of blood" of our ancestors, be it in the slave plantations in the new world or forced labor camps in Africa (206–7). Recognizing the differences in desires of people from the three continents, Fanon articulates three stages of struggle undertaken by the writers who also double as the intellectuals from these communities in the fight for Black people's redemption.

The first stage, the assimilationist phase, is a derivative performance of mimicry of the colonial master's heritage, and a craving for assimilation or, better still, absorption. In the second stage the writer is summarily rejected by the master and feels angry. Consequently, the author begins to recollect and seeks to reconnect with origins and begins to produce literary work that reflects the culture of the author's people. This sort of reactionary art is seen merely as a strategy of diversion, as Edouard Glissant (93–123) suggests, because what emanates from this location of anger and rejection is forced and not natural poetics, for the writer at this moment is still not fully immersed in the struggle with the people. The art is still produced from positions of mental isolationism. The only difference is that it now engages some elements that reflect the European training which hitherto the artist had tended to deny and disparage. In the third stage, the writer finally becomes the voice of awakening for the people to rouse them from their lethargy toward the day of battle. This is what Fanon then calls the fighting literature. It is insurrectionist literature that bellows the nascent fires of resistance and charts the paths to new sociopolitical and cultural beginnings. It is the type of literature the griots performed in the ancient days of epic African heroes such as Mari Djata of Mali, Shaka Zulu, Sunni Ali, and Amina of Zaria, among others.

The art at this point is tied to myth making from the epic journey of the middle passage away from the negating vision of the slave master. There were multiple modes of creative endeavor and codes of dissemination. There were festivals, poetry, narrative lore, and, most especially, performance. August Wilson explains it very succinctly in these words:

> The second tradition occurred when the African in the confines of the slave quarters sought to invest his spirit with the strength of his ancestors by conceiving in his art, in his song and dance, a world in which he was the spiritual center and his existence was a manifest act of the creator from whom life flowed. He then could create art that was functional and furnished him with a spiritual temperament necessary for his survival as property and the dehumanizing status that was attendant to that. (496)

The gradual growth of literacy among African Diaspora peoples in the Americas meant not only a flowering of writing in different genres, but also the ability of these writers to research into the history of Africa that had been hidden from them. Among these genres, drama and performance are most powerful and potentially subversive as they create the illusion of reality on stage. But the type of drama that would help re-vision African Diaspora historical reality had to be different from the type of drama created by European descendants in the Americas. I am not interested at this stage to go into the whole debate about whether African and African Diaspora cultures had drama, a debate made popular by Ruth Finnegan in her foundational text, *Oral Literature in Africa*. Notable theorists such as Isidore Okpewho, Biodun Jeiyifo, Wole Soyinka, Ngugi wa Thiong'O, and August Wilson, among others, have proven otherwise. The defenders of drama in African-derived cultures universally have drawn heavily from elements of theatrical performances found in festivals, rituals, and other cultural celebrations. These elements include myth, dance, music, ritual, and the like, which, as Soyinka puts it, are connected to everyday living yet when performed at the festival grounds become transformed into a more "intense, symbolic and expressive level of reality" (137).

If Soyinka's argument is based on the interruption of the colonial mindset of African and African Diaspora people by uprising cultural textualities, Ngugi wa Thiong'O's argument in "Enactments of Power: The Politics of Performance Space" (in *Penpoints, Gunpoints, and Dreams*) describes how the performance of Itiuka, an Agikuyu festival that predated British colonization of East Africa, suddenly was interpreted as a threat to British colonial rule. Thus, the theatrical elements of myth in the festival challenged directly the use of the myth of cultural superiority to the project of imperialism that Britain was fostering on Kenyan people. As Ngugi wa Thiong'O later asserts, "there is no performance without a goal" (448), a position endorsed by all the participants at the congress in Rome. Subsequently, all drama in the African world is socially committed.

That social commitment is tied to the type of theatre that dramatists of the African world have created from symbiotic adaptations that blend non-African dramatic elements with African and African-derived theatrical elements. But before I plunge precipitously into a discussion of what some of these elements are, it is important to present the case for other

elements that deal with issues of history, land, race, religion, and culture
and how to retrieve these from the falsehoods of Eurocentric propagandist rhetoric. At this point I will describe the path of my initial proposal
from the pinnacle of history as theme and performance. To initiate a
discussion on the importance of history as performance, I appeal to critic
Greg Dening. In *Mr. Bligh's Bad Language*, Dening argues that "history
is not so much fact as performance" (292). Thus, for African Caribbean
and African American playwrights, the most effective way of deconstructing the lie of the nonexistence of African historical contributions to
world civilization must be through theatre and performance. Dramatists
from the African world, then, as Hayden White postulates in *Metahistory:
The Historical Imagination in Nineteenth-Century Europe*, see history
from a new angle. History is no longer "the past; it is the consciousness of
the past used for present purposes" (170).

Understandably, therefore, I read Willis Richardson's *The Dark
Horseman*, Maud Cuney-Hare's *Antar of Araby*, and Aimé Césaire's *And
the Dogs Were Silent* as dramas of radical departure in a reactive project
of cultural substitution. These plays move toward the nurturing of "authentic" African Diaspora voices in the artificially racialized spaces in the
United States and Caribbean cultural, historical, and educational industries. These plays differ remarkably from other collections purporting to
reflect and represent African Diaspora concerns and histories of struggle
in authorship, theme, and performance. But, as Carter Woodson (qtd. in
Hatch and Hill), an eminent African American historian has argued, non-
Blacks cannot sensibly "dramatize Negro life because they misunderstand
the Negro because they cannot think black." In order for African and
African Diaspora life to be truly represented on stage, therefore, they
have to write their own historical and cultural dramas. And this is what
the three dramatists set out to do, and they do it successfully.

Through these plays, Diasporic Africans in the Americas interrogate
traditional Eurocentric racist historiography that has unabatedly sought to
erase African peoples' contributions to world history. These plays challenge the history taught in American and Caribbean schools that defined
the world through historical foreclosure sealed by the written word.
Hence, Africa-centered oral histories that did not fit into the European
paradigm of the written word have been programmatically denied entry
into the market of historical fact and sold at the margins as myth and
fiction. Consequently, and as Helen Gilbert and Joanne Tompkins have

ably argued in *Post-colonial Drama: Theory, Practice, Politics* (107), "history [among colonized peoples, among whom I will place Africans, African Caribbean and African Americans] is re-evaluated and redeployed in post-colonial [insert post-emancipation] drama" not through "historicizing theater productions" but through an examination of how "plays and playwrights construct the discursive contexts for an artistic, social, and political present by enacting other versions of the pre-[modern European] contact period" (107). Gilbert and Tompkins further stress that, in such cases, the colonized people—such as Africans in Africa, the Caribbean, and North America prior to the Harlem Renaissance, the Trinidad Awakening, the Black Arts Movements, the Negritude movements, and the like—seek to reconstruct and tell the other sides of their stories through fragments of historical references (what Derek Walcott called "Fragments of Epic Memory" in his Nobel prize speech) that could and cannot be erased. Reconstructing the past necessarily entails myth, writes James A. Arnold in reference to Edouard Glissant's work. Gissant wrote on "myth, history and literature in the French West Indies in an effort both to establish the grounds for a new Caribbean historiography and to situate myth—especially tragic myth—in this context" (xxvi). Myth making or mythicizing is necessary for the formulation and execution of uprising textualities and voices that challenge the biased empiricism of historical narratives by white North American missionaries, anthropologists, historians, and archaeologists, among others, whose views and interpretations of the histories of Africans collaborated with the European imperial project of world domination.

Granted this is so, Stephen Slemon's (103) position is that "postcolonial *texts* [are pivotal] in the sphere of cultural work and in the promulgation of anti-colonial resistance." Slemon stresses the recognition of the way in which "this social emplacement of the literary text thus affords post-colonial criticism a material reference in social struggle" (103). Positioned this way, I maintain that the plays by Richardson, Hare, and Césaire functionally and ideologically rise above mere anticolonial, antiracist resistance texts toward becoming brazen *cuestionamientos* of Eurocentric (mis)representation of Africans in history. The help creates early mental clearings to provide intellectual culturescapes within which a remapping and renaming of African achievements for the enlightenment of Africans in Diaspora can be envisioned, attained, and sustained. My choice of these plays is determined by the parallels then between the historical treatment of Africans in pre-Islamic and Roman times and the consequences of that treatment on Africans in modern Diaspora. The choice is also recognition of rhetorical and ideological veins that are cultural, historical, economic, social, spiritual, geographical, and racial passwords to logging into African Diaspora genealogies of resistance.

In *The Black Horseman*, *And the Dogs Were Silent*, and *Antar of Araby*, we first encounter what Lhamon refers to as "the optic black mode [through which the African American playwright] enacts and replays the imbrications of Atlantic peoples, the problems they share, and their distinctive pain" (114). Hence, it is reasonable to argue that Cuney-Hare, Césaire, and Richardson refuse to enter into a recycled performance of the most "disdained idioms of black culture and their hardened partisans" (114), in which blackness and whiteness contest each other. Although Lhamon's reading focuses on the shared and almost comparable histories from the 1500s to the present, my focus is on the performance of discursive reclamation of legendary/mythical African figures in what is now read as the Middle East and thus outside of the arena of the United States and the new world of cultural partisanship defined by phenotypic consideration. The heroic figures in *Antar of Araby* and *The Black Horseman* and the tragic hero in *And the Dogs Were Silent* are not conscripted to maintain "optic blackness," but are invoked as allies to journey with African Diaspora people through the agonies of racist historiographies. These plays also demonstrate that Richardson, Césaire, and Cuney-Hare draw on continental African figures, linguistic paraphernalia, and spirituality that predate Christopher Columbus's journey in order to destabilize what Lhamon calls the gravitational pull to optic blackness (115). The fact that the iconic figures drawn in these plays mythicize, present, and perform an African past in which the Africans, either as slaves or vassals, still nonetheless participated in the decisions that affected them or others opens up new arguments in favor of the striving of African Diaspora peoples to become active participants in the political and cultural landscape of the Americas in which they now live. The plays need to be seen as catalytic ingredients for the raising of racial and historical consciousness through providing avenues for racial re-membering.

Notwithstanding the above declarations, the pertinent questions we must confront now are these: How is history performed in these plays? Is it history or myth that is performed? Are the terms "myth" and "history" mutually exclusive? I would say no to the last question and yes to the earlier ones. In these plays, reality is merged between past and present for Diasporic Africans. The three plays dramatize inextricably the intertwined nature of the relationship between Africans under colonial Roman rule, Africans enslaved in pre-Islamic Arabia, and Africans enslaved in the Americas. The relationship is further governed by similar political, economic, class, and racial constructs and hierarchies. Thus, in all these historical periods, Africans either under Arab or European rule have been psychologically marked by prison-like existence, a situation better dramatized by Makak in Derek Walcott's *Dream on Monkey Mountain*. The image of the jail is a symbolic performance of the territorial, individual, and collective deprivations that people of African descent in the new world suffer from. Imprisonment is not just physical containment, but psychological and spiritual enchainment.

But as Ngugi wa Thiong'O says, the prison can ironically also become a performance space of resistance, for it is in only the prison that the colonized can have that liminal space in which to contest the colonizers' power of oppression.

Consequently, in order to break down the prisons and achieve a liberatory existence, the challenge issued by W. E. B. Du Bois (7) was accepted by African Diaspora dramatists. Franz Fanon declares unequivocally that "each generation must out of relative obscurity discover its mission, fulfill it, or betray it" (206–7). Understandably, therefore, Willis Richardson's *Plays and Pageants from the Life of the Negro* became a radical departure in the reactive project of cultural substitution toward the nurturing of "authentic" African American voices in the artificially racialized spaces in cultural, historical, and educational industries in the United States. These plays and pageants differed remarkably from other collections purporting to reflect and represent African American concerns and histories of struggle in authorship, theme, and performance.

Maud Cuney-Hare's *Antar of Araby*, Aimé Césaire's *And the Dogs Were Silent*, and Willis Richardson's *The Black Horseman* are pageants with mythic and epic dimensions. The plays are the deliberate engagement by these authors of nascent African traditions of theatrical performances, which under slavery were banned to the recesses of African Diaspora cultural consciousness. Elements such as the episodic and romantic narrative re-presentation of ideas, the vast geographical spread of the action, and the heroic deeds and nature of the characters in these dramas provide the ritual and mythical spaces in which is enabled the evocation and invocation of African historical figures and events. In addition, the engagement of other performance elements—dance, music, storytelling, riddling, praise poetry, and other folkloric components—shows that both Richardson's and Cuney-Hare's pageants in the 1920s reflect a closer affinity to the conceptual frame of African festival theatre where myth, ritual, and performance always blend.

Another underlying reason that justifies the invocation and evocation of legendary Africans is to center Blacks in center stage as the prime movers and determiners of their lives. The plays initiate a pan-African pan-historical momentum that, as they hoped, would give African Diaspora performances a global circulation and hence provide greater valence and agency to the struggles of African Americans. The plays aimed at invigorating the sapping energies of African Diaspora peoples and hoped to create alternative agendas and genuine territorial mapping in which diasporic Africans could effectively generate a culture of self-representation that would unite their past with their present. The plays deploy the legends of Massanisa, Antar, and a rebel slave as contrapuntal histories that survive in oratures of North Africa and the Arab world, as well as in Caribbean narratives of heroic slave rebellions. Furthermore, the plays reveal a global relationship between Africans everywhere and in every time and explore Black Diaspora anxieties in a globalized context (Stoval 222). In addition, and as Kobena Mercer (142) argues, the plays and pageants by Cuney-Hare, Césaire, and Richardson convert racial politics into anagrammatic new tracings and mappings to resolve the mystery of the silences and silencing of Africans in the new world histories. Hence, the three plays display historical precedence and entanglements of racial and class identities that completely destroy monologic and dialogic stereotypes, especially in the case of Antar, a slave yet from royal loins. Antar's constant mobility from periphery to center and back and forth gives us a glimpse of the cultural and racial anxieties endured by Africans in the Americas.

Accordingly, the plays by Richardson, Césaire, and Cuney-Hare are revolutionary counterdiscourse praxes that seek to celebrate the presence of Africa in the Americas. Furthermore, in *Antar of Araby*, *The Black Horseman*, and *And the Dogs Were Silent*, the performance elements, forms, and contents prefigure much of the practice and politics of what today is conceptualized and defended as exclusively particular to postcolonial dramas. I want to suggest that these plays are carnivals of cultural and historical recall in which the articulation of racial memory is recuperated through performative history. It is hence incumbent on us to interpret them within the second phase of Fanon's historical continuum in which *Antar of Araby, And the Dogs Were Silent,* and *The Black Horseman* are located in the literature of consciousness awakening and thus are forerunners of the literature of warfare and revolutionary engagement that Fanon advocates.

In the preface to *Early Black American Playwrights and Dramatic Writers: A Biographical Directory and Catalog of Plays, Films, and Broadcasting Scripts,* Bernard L. Peterson laments the "gap in the history of the American theatre" as reflected by the "omission or inadequacy of information in most standard reference books on the majority of serious or legitimate Black American playwrights prior to 1950, whose works were produced in hundreds of theatres, community auditoriums, churches, schools, and halls throughout the United States and abroad from the antebellum period to World War II" (xiii). Among these playwrights Maud Cuney-Hare is hardly mentioned because Cuney-Hare was celebrated more for her career as a researcher and promoter of African music forms around the world, especially in the Americas, than as a playwright, hence the neglect of her play, *Antar of Araby.* Indeed, this neglect has been compounded by Cedric Dover, who among other vitriolic comments unfairly attacks Cuney-Hare of plagiarism. But what Dover fails to visualize in his search for creative purity, and not see in Cuney-Hare's act of creative mimicry, is the ideological framework that underpins the dramatic retelling of the history of Antar for the purpose of educating African Americans about great Africans and their contribution to world culture.

Cuney-Hare did not choose an unknown story to graft her play on; instead, she chose the epic of Antara of Arabia, who is more popularly known among scholars of ancient sagas and epic romances as Antara Ibn Shaddad el-Absi: Antar, son of Shaddad, of the tribe of Abs. I am convinced that Cuney-Hare chose to write on Antar for three reasons, which my essay will try to expose. Comparatively, Cuney-Hare's play cannot be equated in quality of verse or narrative brilliance with the original oral narrative, still celebrated in several Arab nations today. However, as Claude McKay puts it in a conversation with Cederic Dover:

> Antar is as great in Arabian literature as Homer in Greek. . . . To me
> the verses of Antar, written more than twelve centuries ago, are more
> modern and full of meaning for a Negro than is Homer. Perhaps if
> black and mulatto children knew more of the story and the poetry of
> Antar, we might have better Negro poets. But in our Negro schools and
> colleges we learn a lot of Homer and nothing of Antar. (89–90)

McKay's statement echoes the challenge thrown out to African American writers of the antebellum period in the *Indianapolis Freeman* of March 2, 1889, calling for the celebration of the great achievements of people of African descent on the American stage. This call originated from the racist, nauseating, and negative stereotypical representation of African Americans in American stage performances. The author felt exasperated with the perpetuation of negative portrayals of the colored folk as people without any historical and cultural achievements, but as a people grounded happily in illiteracy, ignorance, and servitude. The response to this call came through musicals, spectacles, operas, and drama. Through these genres of performance art, African Americans sought to reposition themselves in order to challenge the racist historiography promulgated and enforced through European and white American culture industries such as schools and theatres. W. E. B. Du Bois (7) rejects the charge that African Americans do not appreciate Negro drama. His argument is based on a desire to see good dramatic plays scripted and performed by Blacks for Blacks that sincerely represented their histories, culture, and aspirations:

> If a man writes a . . . good play, he is lucky if he earns first class
> postage upon it. Of course he may sell it commercially to some pro-
> ducer on Broadway, but in that case it would not be a Negro play or if
> it is a Negro play it will not be about the kind of Negro you and I know
> or want to know. If it is a Negro play that will interest us and depict
> our life, experience, and humor, it cannot be sold to the ordinary theat-
> rical producer, but it can be produced in our churches and lodges, and
> halls. (7)

Du Bois's argument is a rejection of the commoditization of Black experience through plays and dramatic productions that target a white audience, who undoubtedly have the money to patronize these productions.

Though *Antar of Araby* appeared in Richardson's *Plays and Pageants from the Life of the Negro*, it falls into the same thematic and ideological paradigm of Richardson's later collection, *Negro History in Thirteen Plays*. This second collection is a panoramic assemblage of the achievements of Africans in contemporary history. Continental African historical figures such as Samory and Menelik are enlisted to prop up the ideological bent of the project. In this latter book, Richardson sought to represent people of African descent around the globe. As W. G. G., a reviewer, proudly wrote, Richardson's enterprise reveals a "modernized Negro [who] is gradually learning to think for himself and to see history from a new point of view" (75). Cuney-Hare through *Antar of Araby* saw her role as that of a builder of an African American culture of historical recuperation, much in the same vein as Richardson's latter collection. Carter Woodson, an eminent historian, also disliked the representation of Blacks by whites in their drama and argued that whites cannot sensibly "dramatize Negro life because they misunderstand the Negro because they cannot think black." In order for Black life to be truly represented on stage, therefore, Blacks had to write their own historical and cultural dramas.

Maud Cuney-Hare's personal and family battles with racism ensured that her choice of *Antar of Araby* did not originate in a lack of imagination but from a subtle intelligence that recognized the parallels between the treatment of enslaved/emancipated Africans and their descendants by pre-Islamic and Islamic Arabs and Christian Europeans in the Americas. Her play, together with others in a similar rhetorical and ideological vein, must be seen as a cultural and racial password for logging into African American genealogies of resistance. In addition, Cuney-Hare's project must have been nurtured by a desire to counter the erroneous representations of Africa as a prelapsarian paradise that was recklessly destroyed by European and Arab barbarism. Rather, as we read the play, we enter into an Africa with its "battles and disagreements that inevitably characterized the time before European" interventions (110). Finally, I posit that Cuney-Hare's play reveals the often-silenced rape of Africa by Arabs, who were major players and beneficiaries in both the trans-Saharan slave trade and the trans–Indian Ocean slave trade.

In order to historicize and contextualize the story in the play, it is necessary to give a brief overview of the perennial interactions between peoples of the Horn of Africa and the Arabian Peninsula. The story of the interactions between western Sudanic peoples, including the Nubians, Ethiopians, and members of other Chadic nations, is well documented.

However, what is now just beginning to emerge are the interactions between Black Africans and nations bordering the Indian Ocean and ancient Egypt. Bearing in mind that pre-Islamic Arabia was surrounded by Ethiopia, Persia, and Byzantium, the most powerful empires of the time, Yemen, which was the dominant peninsular kingdom, had extensive ties with Ethiopia, which had extensive control in the area. These relationships were often very fluid. Thus, as Michael A. Gomez has put it, "Ethiopian incursions [into the Arabian peninsula] are but one example of interaction between the Horn of Africa and Arabia that has existed for millennia; related languages and cultures are another" (46).

> Such interconnectedness suggests that Ethiopians and Nubians made contributions to the Yemeni and Arab gene pool, along with other populations from the Horn. It is therefore no surprise that one of the greatest poets of pre-Islamic Arabia was 'Antara (or 'Antar), son of an enslaved Ethiopian or Nubian mother and an Arab father. Born in the pre-Islamic *jahiliyya* period ("time of barbarism"), 'Antara followed his mother's status and was a slave, but he earned his freedom through military prowess. His background is similar to that of another figure of the early Islamic period, Khufaf Ibn Nadba, son of an Arab father and enslaved black mother who rose to become head of his (Arab) group or "tribe." (46)

These stories, among others, often persuade African Americans, until Darfur, that in the Arab world, "blackness was," or is, "no barrier" (46). Yet, in spite of these individual cases, Gomez argues, there was already a racial bias against Black Africans and their descendants in pre-Islamic Arabia that bloomed into full-scale racism during the Islamic conquest of North Africa and the escalation of the trans-Saharan slave trade. Most Africans who entered into the Arab world came as slave women or boys who were then castrated and served as eunuchs in the harems of the chieftains. Interestingly, however, and unlike their slave counterparts in the Americas, slave children often were considered offspring of their fathers and hence were considered to be born free. This evidence supported Cuney-Hare's ideological challenge impugning white America's historical denial of legitimacy to their biracial children. This created what W. E. B. Du Bois described as "double consciousness" and what Kalpana Seshadri-Crooks addresses in *Desiring Whiteness: A Lacanian Analysis of Race*—a kind of anxiety of existence among diasporic Africans that is measured by mimicry.

This anxiety of existence is revealed through the opening setting: a Syrian suite, a Babylonian suite, and an Arabian suite. As the setting is a royal court or household in which Antar is a slave and his mother is a slave concubine, it is understandable that cultural symbols (music, costume, and the like) would be Arab. Nonetheless, the play's focus is not on these cultural symbols but on the dynamics of the epic struggle by Antar, an allegory of diasporic Africans' search for self-representation, acceptance, and integration in a racist slave and postslave society. Antar's search is heroically performed through drama and performance poetry. The struggle of Antar for legitimation in his father's tribe runs parallel to the struggle of children of biracial liaisons in the Americas under slavery and up to the present. Antar's struggles dramatize the epic nature of the struggles of Africans in the United States for voice and location in the domain of the politically and economically dominant section of their ancestry. Thus, Cuney-Hare's project suggests a comparison between Antar's lamentation and desire to legitimize his birthright through a combination of servility and insubordination, the warrior's reckless bravery, and the poetic sublimity of the romantic dreamer/lover.

The use of the narrator to open the play connects Cuney-Hare's style to what has been described as a provenance of postcolonial dramatists. In using the narrator as griot, Cuney-Hare appropriates narrative and moral authority that recollects her West African ancestral historiographer and raconteur. As griot, an oral historian, such as that played by Djeli Mamoddou Kouyate in *Sundiata: An Epic of Old Mali*, Cuney-Hare in her narrative alter ego purports to report the story of Antar to us verbatim, without changing a word as she received it in translations. Her vision is to continue to tell the story, not as her own but as a way to educate young African Americans about their African past, to enable them to make the right choices in life. Thus, to accuse her of plagiarism, as Dover has done, is to engage a false paradigm for reading the text. Gilbert and Tompkins assert that "[t]he story-teller relayed the community's history, often in verse form, as an entertainment and an educational device. Frequently [also], s/he would augment the narrative with dramatic action, audience interaction, dance, song, and/or music of some description" (120). The narrator thus does not just chronicle facts, but analytically presents them as a guiding post from which to critically engage the texts and contexts of performance through contemporary cross-cultural, racial, and political paradigms in a dynamic and fluid fusion of forms (Rubin 410). Thus, the narrator's introduction of Antar as the "son of the black-faced Zebeeba" (Cuney-Hare 35) foregrounds the historical struggle of descendants of Black Africans in Diaspora for acceptance as equals in a world segregated, categorized, and hierarchized along phenotypes. The pre-Columbian world in which Antar engages his struggle is, through drama, restaged and given newer dimensions that are relevant to African American experience.

The play's subtle manipulation of Antar's story performs a new myth that globalizes African people's perennial struggle for acceptance in a world that has rejected their humanity and great contribution to human history, and has constructed a controlling view of them that ensures servitude. As Gilbert and Tompkins have argued, and drawing from examples of anticolonial and postcolonial dramas from Africa, the role of the storyteller is "one of the most significant manipulations of historical [cultural] narratives in [post]colonial societies" (120). According to them, "Telling stories on stage is an economical way in which to initiate theatre since it relies on imagination, recitation, improvisation, and not necessarily on stage properties. Its place as a strategy for re-visioning history in postcolonial theatre is not based on economics" (126). It is rooted in the position of "maintenance of the group's cultural" heritage (16). In *Antar of Araby* Cuney-Hare recognizes the pivotal roles of women as custodians of historical narratives. Subsequently, she makes Selma and Anis enter the narrative space as interlocutors to supplement and complement the unnamed narrator's role. As insiders to the plot, and as insiders in subservient and marginal locations, they are privileged with the knowledge derived from their inspectorial gaze mounted from that marginalized position, and that allows them to move in and out of the center. The atmosphere of romance is conveyed through the perceptive articulations of an Acadia of un-belonging yet longing to belong. The roles of the storyteller, the scribe, and the two women demonstrate Cuney-Hare's awareness of how orality challenges and demystifies the "naturalistic conventions by which western theatre usually stages the subject matter" (127). Those roles also all help to emphasize the *sankofa* philosophy in which the past is mediated through the present and the present the past toward the construction of the future. In addition to these roles, the presence of the storyteller who narrates yet allows the events she narrates to be enacted for the understanding of the traveler (such as the modern-day African American curious about his past) renders cultural legitimacy to the text. The storyteller educates us on how African American culture is narrated, "(re)constructed," learned, performed, and handed down. By looking into her own community, Cuney-Hare is able to fuse and synthesize the dual dramatic heritage of Europe (style of language used) and Africa (the way language is used and other props) in her play.

Similar to what has been observed in African theatre, the storyteller technique is defined as a metatheatrical device that "draws attention to the relationship between the narrative and its performative enunciation" (Gilbert and Tompkins 127). In this case, Cuney-Hare's use of this theatrical device enables her to affect the audience through the sympathetic relationship between the audience in the play and the external audience sitting in the theatre. The storyteller as cultural retainer is a potential revolutionary as Fatima Dike puts it: "we don't tell bedtime stories to put people to sleep, we want to scare the shit out of them and wake them up" (qtd. in Gilbert and Tompkins 137). By introducing the storyteller and the scribe later, Cuney-Hare blends the two narrative performative traditions prevailing in African American communities and which are traceable to Africa—the oral and the written—but through a relationship in which the oral is given a primary role. I am, however, troubled by the kind of weight given by the king to the scribe later in the story. My worries lie in the ability of the written word, as stated above, to appropriate and claim ownership of a people's voice through the stabilization and foreclosure of nuanced engagements with history as mediated performance.

The oral performance has a built-in mechanism of modifications through narrative mediations. But when that performance is scripted, the former flexibility disappears. Thus, the oral narrator seems to be replaced in favor of a scribe who now must continue to write the story of Antar. In this scribal text, Antar's nobility is engendered in his Arab ancestry, thus foreclosing any possibility of any claim to royalty on his Black mother's side. As the son of a slave mother, it does not matter whether the mother comes from royalty also. In Antar's case this is so. At the end of the play his true nobility is from the father, but from the maternal line. This to me is a bold political statement by Cuney-Hare, who repudiates the racist manner in which all positive aspects of a biracial child are ascribed to the white father or mother. Antar has this to say:

Hail Zeheir, King of the Absians! I have borne the evils of fortune 'till I have garnered its secret meaning. Languishing in the hospitality of Chosroe's Court is a hoary and venerable Ethiopian monarch. From him I learned that Zebeeba, my mother, stolen and enslaved by the tribe of Jeseela was the daughter of a mighty monarch of Ethiopia. Thy glory is my glory. Thy station, my station. (74)

But what type of nobility is he praised for? Is that strain of nobility derived from the maternal or paternal line? Notably, his performance of violent masculinity, which shows his desire to earn social reputation and perhaps earn public respectability in the sociopolitical realm, is mediated and governed by a greater nobility of gentleness, honesty, devotion, faithfulness, and a "penchant for sacrifice and truth" (48–49). This constant swing between the genetic codes in Antar indicates a constant struggle to assert both heritages if only given the chance by his father's people. By inscribing and ringing himself into fiery temper and brazen reckless courage, among other masculinist behavioral patterns, Antar hopes to earn himself entry into his father's world of masculinity and power. But his poetic prowess is derived from his mother's people, not his Arab fathers. Consequently, in the short dialogue between the Stranger and the Scribe, the Stranger confesses that "In blackness there is some virtue, if you observe its beauty well" (37). He goes on to further elucidate his point through contrastive analysis of the role of blackness in the appreciation of beauty. This line of thought resonates with what I raised earlier about the polemic of colorism that characterizes African American cultural politics.

Nonetheless, these praises of blackness are structured on categories in which phenotypes are taken as measures of character, or, as Homi Bhabha puts it, "signs [are] taken for wonders." The outsider location of the Stranger, his obsessive curiosity about Antar, prefigures and predicts African Americans' thirst for knowledge about the great heroes of Africa. The scribe's reflective intervention to the stranger's patronizing and essentialized exultation of Antar's qualities is disturbing when we sift through the nuances of his description of Antar's mother. In this narrative, Shedad, Antar's biological father, is presented as "the noble leader" who discovered "the tribe of Jezela—a tribe of great riches. Between the hills was a Black woman grazing her camels. She was uncommonly beautiful and alluring, and made a great impression on the heart [loins] of Shedad. She was completely hid in her hair, which appeared like the dark shades of night" (36–37). According to Roland Oliver and Anthony Atmore in *Medieval Africa: 1250–1800* (115), women from this part of Africa were known for their beauty and were often raided and carried off as concubines or wives by Arabs. But history apart, the fact that Antar's mother is an unfathomable, almost surreal creature that must be possessed and explored, like the idea of dark Africa that must be penetrated, explored, and conquered, is suggestive. I do not wish to overstretch this symbolic relationship between Shedad's view of Zebeeba and the views held by Arab and European imperialists about Africa as a continent of great wealth that needs exploitation by her conquerors. Zebeeba at this point is tending her animals and also has a husband and two other children. Black Africa then, like this woman, is beautiful, with lush vegetation, undulating and awe-inspiring terrains, populated by her children, but her paradise must be destroyed for the sake of sating the lust of the Arab or European as is the case with the transatlantic slave trade and later colonization.

Antar of Araby goes beyond recapitulation of historical events in exotic distances to a transcultural and transnational rendition of the historical realities that have defined African Diaspora experiences. Antar's constant cry is for acceptance and legitimation in his father's home as a son. In both pre-Islamic and Islamic cultures, the son of a slave woman was free if his father was a free Arab. In Antar's case, his so-called noble father does not deem it fit to accept his responsibility and give his son the identity he has earned genetically and through honorable and brave conduct in service of the nation. He rescues Shedad's Arab wife and the royal maidens, including Abla and Selma, from bandits singlehandedly. Yet for this singular act of patriotism he is berated by the father even as he is praised by the heir apparent, Prince Malik, and the king himself. Likewise, we have stories of African slaves who defended their masters against the British and against the Union army but never got the adoption into American citizenship that they craved until the 1960s. There is also the parallel narrative of white slaveowners fathering children with their female slaves but then refusing to acknowledge these children as their children, preferring instead to turn these children into slaves by stressing a uterine line of descent since that suited the white master. We also need to remember that African Americans fought and died to protect the white race in both Europe and North America, only to be denied citizenship in the politics of national culture at home.

Similarly, Antar's boldness in war is matched by his oratures. He is also bold and brilliant in tongue. His poetry of love, considered to be among the world's greatest compositions of romance poetry, is testimony to the indubitable role of African American cultural productions such music, dance, poetry, fiction, spirituality, and oratory in the development of America's contribution to world literature and culture. Antar's poetry codifies his thoughts and metaphors of desire and frustration. The language and tone of his performance evokes admiration from all except Robab, the mother of Abla, whose racism is so blatant that it blinds her to Antar's heroic qualities. To Robab, it is unthinkable that Antar, a Black man, should even dare to yearn for her daughter whose "face is like the full moon of heaven, allied to light" (48). In addition to Robab is Sulaymah who conspires with Amarah to have Antar murdered. We are all too aware of the history of lynching based on the false and racist notion that white women needed protection from Black males. Here one questions the so-called nobility of Shedad. Similarly, African American experiences at the hands of European American slave masters and subsequent segregationist ideology question the politics of white cultural and moral superiority in the world. African Americans are equally the sons and daughters of America, and by their blood and sweat the nation is kept safe.

According to historical accounts, African slaves in the Arab world often found themselves in the service of the military, domestic servitude, and the like. There is such a close connection between the way Africans in the Arab world and Africans in the Americas were and are perceived and treated. Thus, Shedad, who should be rejoicing that his son has won all the accolades from the king and has been elevated to sit with him all the time, is shockingly enraged with jealousy. He tells his brother, Sulaymah; "O son of my father and mother, my soul is greatly vexed. Some disturbance, I fear, will arise through the tribe and my blood will be demanded and our persons pay the forfeit" (50–51). To this the evil brother replies: "O my brother, thou hast hit the mark and if thou dost not take measure to put him to death, he will surely endanger our lives" (51). The irony is that it is Antar's bravery and devotion to service that has kept them alive up to now. Cuney-Hare insinuates a rethinking of white America's policy of criminalizing the actions and honest aspirations of African Americans by the state through racial profiling. This has led to unequal incarceration of African Americans even though a larger percentage of them also are wearing the military uniform to keep America safe. Shedad even rejects appeals from Prince Malik, who reminds him that Antar is noble because "he is of thy loins, reject him not, for truly he belongs to thee" (51).

As a result of Prince Malik's prompting, Shedad pretends to be anxious to listen to Antar's request. But when Antar says that he wants to be raised to the "rank and dignity of an Arab [substitute American], acknowledge me as thy son and thyself as my father, so that my rank may be known" (52), Shedad becomes enraged and tells Antar not to be presumptuous because the king has given him robes of honor for his loyalty and bravery, but to remember his slave origins (52). In Shedad, we see a representation of hypocrisy on stage. Cuney-Hare draws upon this ancient romance of Antar to comment on present-day realities of African Americans' struggle to be accepted as true Americans. Shedad, Sulaymah, Amarah, and Robab foreshadow American white supremacists and segregationist establishments that fought against the civil rights of African Americans with the argument that to give equal opportunities to Blacks would be to yield the nation to them and thereby lead to a collapse of white civilization. King Zoheir's proclamation (53) that elevates Antar is symbolically linked to Abraham Lincoln's emancipation proclamation, which was still resisted by white supremacists. It is interesting that the words used by Amarah to taunt Antar—"Black skin, thou lookest vastly miserable indeed" (54)—sound like they were lifted from the African American experience.

Antar then sings his songs of sorrow, what has been described as blues music in America. The lamentations are as powerfully structured and rendered as the poetry of love composed for Abla and the victory songs of self-praise before confronting or after defeating his enemies: "I am the slave of whom it shall be said that I encountered a thousand free-born heroes; my heart was created harder than steel, how then can I fear sword or spear? I will sacrifice myself for the tribes with the long spear until it be honored and respected" (48). He also praises himself before Robab (42). In response, Amarah launches into self-praise as a counterdiscourse to Antar's praise song of himself. But while Antar's poetry of praise is derived from his achievements and is universally recognized and praised by others, Amarah's self-adulation has no public foundation in action. Thus he says: "To-day will I exhibit my valor and courage, the warrior and the horseman shall stand in awe of me. Abla shall mark the deeds of a ferocious lion. When it is all over with that infernal slave, I shall be glorified among Arabs!" (49). Amarah's bravery is not for saving the kingdom but for killing the hero of the kingdom, an argument often used by supremacists who believe they will be rewarded for violent crimes against African Americans. The kind of verbal challenge issued here echoes African oral traditions in which boasting is engaged as a tool of warfare before a real joining of battle with the enemy. We find this in the Sundiata epic and other epics of Africa such as the Mwindi epic from the Kongo. There is also the African American tradition of the Dozens or what is known as bombast or halo poetry. Thus, in *Antar of Araby*, Cuney-Hare gives us an honest rendition of African oral performance. Oratory as dramatic performance is not new to Africans or African Americans, or, by extension, to Afro-Asians. The dramatization of his emotions through bombast, a style of oratorical performance, lifts the play from being a simple play to being a drama of the epic struggles of Africans in transnational locations for inclusion into the national histories of the nations their blood and toil have helped to create. Love is then engaged as a backdrop for this struggle. The language used by Antar is corollary to a choreographed linguistic dance, a dance of the sound of jazz and blues and soul and hip-hop, work songs and spirituals, protest and celebration all in one. Thus, Antar's constant switching from the language of elevated romance to that of victory songs and songs of sorrow (59–60) or boastful challenge must be read as a discursive strategy to represent his complexity as a person and the complexity of his situation.

In reading Shiboob's conversation with Antar, Cuney-Hare takes the play to another dimension. Shiboob is the African brother of Antar and has no pretenses of ever becoming Arab, as he is the son of an African father. He is the slave brought over from Africa to the Americas while Antar is the slave born in captivity. His presence in Antar's life when he is at his lowest is to give him courage and support. Cuney-Hare at this juncture turns the personal lament of Antar into the political and the racial: "Among themselves they call me the son of Zebeeba, but in the tumultuous rush of horsemen, I'm the son of nobles" (59). Thus in time of national calamity like war, the African American is a true patriot, a true American, but in time of peace and prosperity, she is an unwelcomed immigrant. In this critical recognition of his liminality, he is nevertheless pulled toward seeking integration and assimilation through marriage. He is the model slave, the model minority who wants to be given the status of an honorary white. He is no Uncle Tom, though, for he is not a servile, obedient servant who will not stand up for his rights.

Willis Richardson's *The Black Horseman* is a project of dramatic recuperation of African historical fights for survival similar to Cuney-Hare's *Antar of Araby*. Richardson's play is a performance that resembles a talismanic memory defense against historical denials in a world of competing cultural and racial histories. It is the type of epic narrative with drama that griots performed and still perform that celebrates African epic and historical figures such as Sundiata, Shaka, Sunni Ali, Amina of Zaria, Samori, and Nzinga, among others. Because drama can be a powerful creative genre that brings the illusion of reality on stage, it can also be a subversive instrument in the hands of cultural and historical retrievers in the African Diaspora. Likewise, Ngugi wa Thiong'O, in "Enactments of Power: The Politics of Performance Space" (in *Penpoints, Gunpoints, and Dreams*), has stressed that "there is no performance without a goal"; thus, all drama in the Africa Diaspora is socially and politically committed. If this is the case then, my interest in the elements of history and race, and how African Diaspora playwrights seek through drama to retrieve these from negative anti-Africa propagandist representations, is not misplaced but is of utmost urgency toward a fuller understanding of African Diaspora drama and theatre. Greg Dening in *Mr. Bligh's Bad Language* has contended that "history is not so much fact as performance" (292). Thus, for African Diaspora playwrights, the most effective way of deconstructing the lie of the nonexistence of African historical contribution to world civilization must be through theatre and performance. Dramatists must see history from a new angle. History is no longer "the past; it is the consciousness of the past used for present purposes" (170). Moreover, as Larry Neale had proposed, the incestuous idea of art for art's sake that had engaged the mindset of Europe in the nineteenth century was not to be accepted by Black playwrights. Instead, Black playwrights had to position their art in such a way that it becomes the "aesthetic and spiritual sister of the Black power concept," because "both concepts are nationalistic" (Gayle 293).

Understandably, therefore, I want to read Willis Richardson's *The Black Horseman* as a drama of radical though romanticized departure in a reactive and recuperative project of historical substitution toward the nurturing of "authentic" African Diaspora voices in the artificially racialized spaces in cultural, historical, and educational industries in the United

States. This play, though glossing over some historical realities of the time, follows in the footprints of earlier historical plays such as *Dessalines*, *Senegambian Carnival*, *The Sultan of Zulu*, *In Dahomey*, *Abyssinia*, and Du Bois's *The Star of Ethiopia*. Alain Locke had advocated the engagement of "ancestral sources of African life and traditions." For, as he articulated it, it was not possible for anyone "with a sense of dramatic values [to] underestimate the rich resources of African material in these respects. Not through a literal transposing but in some adaptation of its folklore, art idioms, and symbols, African material seems likely to influence the art of drama" (125–26). In addition, Carter Woodson also argued that non-Blacks cannot sensibly "dramatize Negro life because they misunderstand the Negro because they cannot think black." If African Diaspora history and life were to be truly represented on stage, therefore, African Diaspora writers would have to write their own historical and cultural dramas. Thus, in 1935, Willis Richardson and May Miller published their book *Negro History in Thirteen Plays* that sought to dramatize African history.

In these plays, African American dramatists contested traditional Euro-American historiography that sought to erase African history through what James Hatch labeled the "double bind of racism with its double vision of the African as a noble/savage . . . in the commercial theatre of the time" (17). Evidently, Richardson's plays showed an ideological bias toward Africa and African historical achievements. As Bernard L. Peterson Jr. asserts in "Willis Richardson: Pioneer Playwright," many of Richardson's plays were "unique in their glorification of the Black hero long before the world was to affirm that 'Black is Beautiful.' Richardson was one of the first Black playwrights to write romantic plays of Black history dramatizing the lives of such heroes as Crispus Attucks, the first martyr of the American Revolution . . . and Massanisa, King of East Numidia" (Richardson 114). In his review of the main currents in historical writings by African Diaspora people, Orlando Patterson recognized three main groups of thought: the catastrophic, the contributionist, and the survivalist. What Patterson failed to perceive were the revisionists or recuperationists, among whom I count Willis Richardson, whose dramas of African historical figures fall into this category.

Thus, Carter G. Woodson wrote in the introduction to *Negro History in Thirteen Plays* that Richardson and his compatriots had the "vision of the Negro in the new day" and "undertook to dramatize every phase of his life and history" in which the concept of the task "shows no restriction to any particular period or place. The Negro is presented as a maker of civilization in Africa, a contributor to progress in Europe, and a factor in the development of Greater America." He stipulates further that Richardson has definitely proved that the Negro has "something to dramatize, and in spite of mocking onlookers, he has the courage to undertake the task" (Introduction to Richardson and Miller v). In effect, then, *The Black Horseman* seeks to dramatize Massinissa's strategic alliance with the Roman general Scipio to secure survival for himself and expansion for his kingdom. Looked at this way, Massinissa's action in allying himself with Rome, an enemy of Africa, can be interpreted in several ways. My role here is not to trace all the various ways one can read Massinissa's action; rather, I want to see it from the position of the survivalist. A survivalist in an anticolonial and antineocolonial struggle obviously seems traitorous, but in the play and in the historical reality from which the play derives its plot and characters, we can read Massinissa's action in a much more sympathetic light. First, his response to Eubonius's introductory remarks:

> The whole world knows that Massinissa is
> A strong ally of Rome; Syphax of Carthage
> And both those nations hope for power here
> In Africa. Now Massinissa is
> A mighty arm on which Scipio depends,
> An arm without which Roman power here
> Is close to nothing, really less than nothing.
> What if that right arm should be maimed by Syphax? (182)

In this statement lies the main conflict of the play. The political battleground is found in the Roman empire's struggle with Carthage in the Punic Wars for the control of Africa. But to do so, both these nations need the support of Eastern Nubia, ruled by Massinissa. One would think that, because Carthage is an African nation that has dared to confront and challenge the imperial interests of Rome, another African nation would help her neighbor in a show of solidarity to stop the march of Rome. Yet that is not the case.

Massinissa was not interested in having either Rome or Carthage as supreme overlords in Africa. Both had similar ambitions to dominate Africa, and so his constant strategy was to shift his alliances when it became contingent and appropriate to the survival and sustainability of

his kingdom as a strong independent nation. Of course, as history testifies, Massinissa also had expansionist ideas. A weaker Rome and Carthage, caused by their warring rivalry, would mean a strong Numidia. The
two security guards represent the competing views of Africa's place in
world history and politics of the past. On the one hand, Claudius is
suspicious of any African leader's ambitions for political dominance and
alliances as a means of self-preservation. Eubonius, on the other hand, is
represented as the ultra Africanist who would rather have an African rule
the world than a foreigner from Rome (182–85). This is spelled out more
powerfully by Syphax:

> I know you have admired Sophonisba,
> But Hasdrubal, her father, favors me;
> Yet more than favoring me he yearns for power—
> Power to equal Rome's. By you alone
> Of all in Africa can he obtain
> The power he yearns for. (192)

In order to foster an alliance against Rome, Carthage then engages
Syphax, a sworn enemy of Massinissa and an unreliable ally who earlier
had sided with Rome against Carthage but is now linked with Carthage
against Rome, to approach Massinissa with a marriage proposal to Sophonisba, Hasdrubal's daughter. Through the marriage, Massinissa is promised de-elevation to the level of a mere prince of Carthage, while Numidia
transfers to Carthage. As Syphax puts it clearly:

> There's reason in it. Beautiful Sophonisba,
> Princess of Carthage then would be your bride;
> And Hasdrubal, her father, king of Carthage—
> You see, you have hope of being king. (192)

But Massinissa sees through the emptiness of the offer and counters thus:
"What glory's in hope of being king / To one who is a king?" (195). He
also asserts quite correctly that "no kingdom is more powerful than Numidia" (195), and hence he is unwilling to betray his kingdom for the
love of a woman who is merely being used as an object of dynastic
exchange. This testament of fact and confidence underscores his actions.
Numidia's greatness as defined here, a definition that neglects historical
reality, does not lie in expansionist ideology but is negotiated through the
mechanics of survival by playing one rival against the other. The alternative sought by Hasdrubal is one in which Numidia's freedom is jeopard-

ized. He has to "renounce the kingdom of Numidia / To become a prince in Carthage and later King" (193). Massinissa's rejection of the plot of Hasdrubal and Syphax is couched in the language of metaphor:

> Your offer is a cup full of hope,
> But with a drop of poison in it, Syphax.
> That "King of all Numidia" is the poison
> That may pollute the cup; and yet I'll think
> And you may take my answer back with you. (193)

Both Syphax and Hasdrubal are conscious of Massinissa's fierce spirit of independence and his desire to keep his kingdom and people independent, even if it means siding with the continental enemy for a while. In pushing Massinissa to accept the marriage proposal to Sophonisba, whom he loves, even though both Syphax and Hasdrubal know that Hasdrubal would prefer her to marry Syphax, Massinissa is confronted with a political and social dilemma. If Massinissa agrees to the dubious proposal, Hasdrubal will annex the more powerful of the two Numidias and thus be able to continue to contest the supremacy of Rome in Africa even as his brother Hannibal is doing the same in Europe.

> I choose to keep the kingdom of Numidia,
> I choose to keep our pact with Rome, but most
> Of all I choose to hold as something sacred
> The trust of those who love me as their king. (199)

Thus, Massinissa chooses the love for his country and people against his personal love of Sophonisba, described as the most beautiful woman of the then known world. He chooses to defend and uphold the history and survival of his people. Syphax fails to persuade Massinissa in this initial phase and then devises another plot to try to twist the arm of Massinissa to agree to marry Sophonisba. He sends a spy to Massinissa claiming that Scipio, the Roman general, had sent him to tell Massinissa to go ahead and marry Sophonisba. This new plot, if it worked, would then cast doubts on Massinissa's reliability as an ally and a selfless leader of his people, and make Rome attack East Numidia, thus leaving Carthage and West Numidia once again free to be powerful. The spy is found out and tortured to confess.

In making these decisions, Massinissa does not rely solely on his own personal wisdom and imperious ambition. Richardson shows that survival and freedom of the Black African world cannot be achieved and maintained without the total recognition of the wisdom of African women. Thus, during Syphax's visit, the women act as spies and advisers to Massinissa. When we hear the women lament that "A message from Massinissa to Sophonisba / A message from Massinissa to Hasdrubal" (186), they are fully aware that their happiness and the future of Black Numidia depends on Massinissa's response to Syphax's proposal (186). "More than my happiness depends on this; / Numidia's future, Massinissa's honor, / The peace of all of us, our very lives" (188). The women are the agents that not only head-on recognize Syphax's plan to give away his fiancée in order to annex a kingdom but also recognize the way race is engaged in the whole drama of political maneuvering. Consequently, both Casintha and Bosioba cannot accept that white Sophonisba can be good for Black Numidia.

Bosioba:

Imagine Sophonisba ruling here;
The pale, white, Carthaginian Sophonisba
With yellow hair, blue eyes and bloodless limbs

Casintha:

The cold, white, passionless Princess Sophonisba
With a cold heart and a mind that thinks for Carthage. (188)

These comments, racist and stereotypical as they seem, must be seen in the context of African American historical experience up to the 1930s and read from a Fanonian perspective. The image of the white woman as a trophy of Black masculinity is challenged here. Thus, through the interpretation of the intelligence report from Casintha, the women come to the conclusion that there cannot be any real good from a marriage of Black Numidia and white Carthage. It may also be Richardson's way of indicating that the historical and cultural gaps between white people and Black people in America is so vast that Black people stand to lose if they inadvertently and unwisely give away their inheritance to become second-class citizens. Richardson shows that it is dangerous to give away Black heritage in order to be accepted as an honorary white in a political game marked by racial undertones. Thus, as Bosioba says: "How would you fare at the hands / Of Carthage who might scorn a king turned prince?" (197). In addition, Richardson uses the voiced reason of the women to persuade Massinissa that his plan of action is the right one:

Casintha:

Sire, do not grant it. Think a moment, Sire,
Of how your people love you, think of how
Your soldiers fought to give you power here
In Africa, the nation's treasure house.

Bosioba:

Think of the strangers you would tarry with,
Then think of us, your own dark women who
Love you as they love life; but most of all
Think of a pale, cold bride whose kisses are
But shadows of a kiss, whose love would be
An empty dream of love, and give him "no"
For an answer to take back to Hasdrubal. (194)

Through the women Richardson also enjoins us to recognize how survival depends on re-visionary histories and counterdiscourses. He urges us to see that a fanatical adherence to the rules made by the powerful to keep the powerless in check is detrimental to the survival and happiness of the oppressed—in this case, African Americans in a racialized and classed sociopolitical landscape. And he emphasizes that wisdom lies in knowing how to manipulate rules and negotiate through the intricacies of sociopolitical and cultural histories.

Bosioba:

The twisting of the truth into a lie
A broken word, the listening at the door,
May save a kingdom and bring happiness;
While a too rigid clinging to the rules
Of "thou shall not do this," "shalt not do that,"
May bring eternal sorrow, utter woe. (190)

Here we see how Bosioba is the mouthpiece of Richardson. Unless African Americans use all kinds of techniques to bring down the technicalities of the laws arrayed against them, they will forever remain oppressed because the enemy does the same.

The appeal of the women to Massinissa is predictive of the lament of African American females at the seeming lack of solidarity between them and their men. The potential of a united African people is often undermined by the successful Black males accepting honorary roles in a white-dominated economic, political, and cultural landscape through a trophy white wife. The play also casually hints at the allegorical struggle between Black culture and white culture with the women as the metaphors in this struggle. It is Richardson's way of exploring the issue of double consciousness that Du Bois so ably defined in *The Souls of Black Folk* and Fanon described in *Black Skin, White Masks*. In relation to this, the role of Sophonisba demonstrates that, in this contest for the souls of Black men, the white woman tends to always seem to win out because in most cases they come to the contest already loaded with sociopolitical and economic advantage that are used as bait to lure the Black male away from his women, and thus his nation and people. The issue of scorn is important here also. For both Casintha and Bosioba and to some extent Massinissa, to be lured away is not only an act of betrayal but will also bring scorn on such a male and by extension his whole group.

In spite of the fact that this play essentializes, objectifies, and commodifies the white female as mere body without substance, Richardson wants to show that a marriage to Sophonisba—and, by extension, a successful Black male's marriage to a white female—becomes a journey of ostracism because the illusion of power and social mobility and acceptability becomes an entrapment that yields social, economic, cultural, and political decline. The women are honest in their confessed concern for Massinissa's response. "We are concerned for all, your majesty, / For you, Numidia, Africa and ourselves" (195). Through Massinissa's rhetorical question, "And you think I should weaken Africa, / Enslave Numidia, myself and you / If I should wed the Carthaginian Princess" (195), Richardson argues that in an America of his time where normative behavior and legislation support racial inequality, assimilation through interracial marriage reduces the position of Blacks and is detrimental to Black people. Thus, through Massinissa, Richardson argues that the future of the Black nation in America, and indeed for Africans worldwide, depends on racial and cultural unity guided by their history. Personal ambition should always be put aside for the sake of the larger dream of African peoples.

In this play, Richardson gives Massinissa a more symbolic role than the one given in the historical account of him. In his rejection of Sophonisba for the sake of East Numidia, Massinissa ensures the survival of his kingdom. In the reality of history, his personal ambition is to have both Sophonisba and West Numidia. Thus, by allying with Rome, he achieves both. In historical narratives, not only does Massinissa gain Sophonisba when he storms Syphax's palace, but in order to save her from being sent to Rome and paraded in a cage, he marries her but shortly afterward encourages her to commit suicide as a demonstration of solidarity against Rome. Thus, while ostensibly working with the enemy, Massinissa also is able to secure his freedom and that of his people. By allying himself with Rome, he manages to expand his kingdom and bring peace and prosperity until his death at over ninety years. The historical Massinissa is master of intrigue, bravery, and expansionist ideals. Richardson is not interested in this kind of history but in the use of history to teach African American kids to use wisdom to negotiate multiple alliances without being weakened. In this selective dramatization of a particular phase in the long and glorious reign of Massinissa he does not focus on Hannibal, the celebrated Carthaginian general, but on a Black Numidian king. Thus, Richardson is not unselective in his choices of heroes of the African past. His choices are defined by race and informed by the rhetoric of racial and historical retrieval. Thus, the play's action can be read as an allegory in which Massinissa transcends his individual physical and historical reality into the realm of the legend. In thus appearing to collaborate with Rome, Massinissa actually then may be understood to have engaged in a subtle act of resistance to both Carthaginian and Roman agendas, for after the fall of Carthage and the expansion of East Numidia to include West Numidia and parts of Carthage, Massinissa's Numidia becomes a vast kingdom that Rome had to respect.

We now turn to storytelling as the more intricate dramaturgic element. I say intricate on account of the ability of narrative to draw the characters in the play and the audience into a conspirational intimacy, which creates an alienation effect that draws the audience into the act. In all four plays, the role of storytelling fulfills a role different from narrative summary often used to depict events offstage in European drama. Here storytelling is part of the drama. Take for instance, *And the Dogs Were Silent*, in which there are multiple narrators at different stages of the action. The drama starts with Echo, a reflective and critical introduction of the main issues that are performed in the history of the evolution of the Antillean African. Following Echo's introductory warning to the blue-eyed archi-

tect of a pestilential world into which the African has been flung in the
Caribbean are the voices of Narrator, Narratress, First Madwoman, and
Second Madwoman. The narrative presence of these characters gives the
events a verisimilitude that borders on a prophetic representation of history. In African storytelling traditions narrative is enhanced and rendered
immediate in its effectiveness through dramatic representation of the
events narrated. This then enables both the story and the action to create
an atmosphere of total drama. The Madwomen, Narrator and Narratress,
and Chorus and Semichorus become the observers yet also the silent
participants of rebellion through a constancy of their subversive lamentations in which they utter prophecies of rebellion, resistance, and survival
of the Afro-Caribbean people. Thus, their roles are similar yet different
from their counterparts in European drama. For instance, the two madwomen are not comic characters. They are seers, a role that is sometimes
credited to madness in African culture. Thus their language is that of
prophecy. Through them the mysteries of nature and the coming Arma-
geddon in the valley of false peace created by Europe are unraveled
through symbolic language (10). They also prophesy regeneration of the
spirit of rebellion in the ashes of destruction (14), thus indicating that the
desire for freedom by the African in the Antilles cannot be suppressed
forever even if rebellion after rebellion is crushed by the European ma-
chines of war.

Afrocentric dramaturgy is often governed by the performance of narrative through dance and mime. The dances performed in all four plays
help consolidate the oral narratives of song and storytelling. Dance becomes the movement from a position of physical stasis to one of somatic
fluidity, a kinetic release that frees the spirit from the constraints of space
and helps the dancer transcend physicality to enter into the territory of
rebelliousness against control. In these dance performances we see history reenacted and stories told toward energizing the people, the audience
into action. Dance movements often simulate war moves, and thus revolt
is choreographed through dance. Dance also enables the oppressed populations in Africa, the Caribbean, and the United States to exorcize the
demons of doubt and self-hate and also to create fear among the oppressor. Dance has the benefit of multiple interpretations.

Similarly, if, as noted above, song and storytelling and dance are
powerful dramaturgic elements, the role of African-derived worship and
spirituality and their ritual enactments, even if represented on stage, is

also central to the spirit of dramatic representation of African and African diasporic struggles. Nonetheless, we must also take note to what Walcott in "What the Twilight Says: An Overture" says about this kind of appropriation of traditions that have somehow lost their potency. He argues that the African phase entered by Caribbean poets, carvers, and dramatists is pathetically hollow because what they produce lacks the spirit and passion of the real. He states that for Afro-Christians, African gods are no longer a force. "We could pretend to enter [their] power but [they] would never possess us, for our invocations [are] not prayer but devices. The actor's approach could not be catatonic but rational, expository, not receptive . . . all we could successfully enact [is] a dance of doubt" (8–9). Rebel takes this lamentation up in Act II of *And the Dogs Were Silent* (26–28). Without doubt European representations of Christianity enabled them to colonize Africans and also became the spiritual and moral justification of slavery and oppression. The Bible always preceded the gun in the modern history of the European-ruled world. To mount a successful rebellion, therefore, the writers of these plays had three choices. One option is to side with the oppressor and his interpretation of what Christ preached. We find this in wa Thiong'O's satirized lamentation of the way in which Christianity becomes an effective tool of neocolonialism. For those who became born-again Christians, limited access is granted to the corridors of power through land grants and shares in the exploitative factories in Kenya. Thus, Christianity, which was a tool of colonization, now becomes a tool of neocolonial oppression. In *All the Dogs*, Christianity is represented by the corrupt, pornographic, and morally bankrupt bishop who consorts with the agents of colonization (9). In *All the Dogs*, Rebel rejects all religion. He laments that he has called on the gods of Africa and they do not answer him, so he aligns himself to another European ideological invention, Marxism, which uses European scientific rationalism as a discourse on freedom.

The Rebel learns that in a bitter manner. In *All the Dogs* Césaire adopts a pro-Marxist discourse and strategy as the only solution to the problems of slavery, colonialism, and neocolonial oppression. In this, African Caribbean cultural practices are ironically sidestepped or mocked and replaced by a Eurocentric ideology that goes against the African's spiritualized worldview. Césaire misrepresents African communalism as communism/socialism without considering the historical roots of Marxist ideology. Hence his play ends with defeat, defeat of the Rebel, defeat of revolution, because Césaire, like his compatriots, did not truly believe in a cultural revolution that promoted Africa. Thus, Césaire also shows he has no belief even in socialism and that violence as a tool to overthrow the oppressor's violent rule will ultimately end in futile sacrifice as the people abandon Rebel. Here, we see Césaire's initial and perpetual disagreement with Fanon, who holds that sometimes violence becomes the best strategy to overthrow violence. In the end, all these plays show uncertain futures. The plays continue the debates and enliven the views and voices articulated from the 1890s African Diasporas, voices that became more pronounced in the 1950s Black Power, Negritude, and independence movements in the African world. They continue the call for cultural and political and historical and aesthetic action against the colonizer externally and internally. Thus, in *All the Dogs Were Silent*, we are confronted with failed revolution as an answer to Fanon and Amiri Baraka.

Throughout this chapter I have endeavored to show how Cuney-Hare, Richardson, and Césaire all engage certain dramaturgical devices such as song, dance, poetry, narrative, ritual, and other African-derived performance elements to create new myths out of old ones and to give the African slave's voice the same status as the royal's. In all three plays, there is the epic struggle by the African to counter the imperialism of the outsider. Race and class are very important factors in these dramas of struggle. Though in both Cuney-Hare's and Césaire's plays the heroes are slaves, Cuney-Hare's is historically grounded in a real person while Césaire's is a nameless hero who nonetheless rises to become an allegory of all the tragic slave rebellions in the Americas. Antar is also related to *The Black Horseman* because he and Massinissa are both royal. I have also argued for an appreciation of the griot qualities of the raconteur, the engagement of linguistic devices that reflect African, African American, and Afro-Arab use of language as powerful tools for self-articulation. Moreover, I have linked the historical experiences of African slaves in the Arab world to that of Africans in the Americas. Finally, writing among diasporic Africans is a revolutionary act, thus in *Antar of Araby*, when the king orders the scribe to write everything down carefully for posterity, we must see the urgency of this edict for the writers in the African Diasporas. Writing must originate from a revelatory desire to give descendants of Africans in diasporic locations a historical sense of self-worth despite the low status they may occupy on the economic, political, social, and racial ladders. Thus, the story of *Antar of Araby*, the story of Massinissa, and the stories of heroic slave revolt leaders must be recorded in hieroglyphics of performance drama and poetry as testimony of hope, faith, self-forgiveness, and love. The political subtleties of Rebel, Antar, and Massinissa are brought to life on stage and through that made into myth through the scribe's skills. African people's histories are thus rendered more truthfully through performance that in its global appeal enters into the realm of epic/myth.

WORKS CITED

Arnold, James A. "Introduction." *Aimé Césaire Lyric and Dramatic Poetry*. Trans. Clayton Eshieman and Annette Smith. Charlottesville: UP of Virginia, 1990. xi–xli. Print.

Ayejina, Funso. "The Death and Rebirth of African Deities in Edward Kamau Brathwaite's *Islands*." *WLWE* 23.2 (1984): 397–404. Print.

Baraka, Amiri. "The Revolutionary Theatre." *The Norton Anthology of African American Literature*. Ed. Henry Louis Gates Jr. and Nelley Y. McKay. 2nd ed. New York: W. W. Norton, 1996. 1960–63. Print.

Bhabha, Homi. "Signs Taken for Wonders. Questions of Ambivalence and Authority under a Tree Outside Delhi, May 1817." *The Location of Culture*. London: Routledge, 1994. 102–22. Print.

Césaire, Aimé. *And the Dogs Were Silent. Aimé Césaire Lyric and Dramatic Poetry 1946–82*. Trans. Clayton Eshleman and Annette Smith. Charlotteville: UP of Virginia, 1999. 3–74. Print.

Cuney-Hare, Maud. *Antar of Araby*. *Plays and Pageants from the Life of the Negro*. Ed. Willis Richardson. Jackson: UP of Mississippi, 1993. Print.

Dening, Greg. *Mr. Bligh's Bad Language: Passion, Power and Theatre on the Bounty*. Cambridge: Cambridge UP, 1992. Print.

Dike, Fatima. Keynote address at the International Women Playwright's Conference, Adelaide, Australia, July 4, 1994. Quoted in Helen Gilbert and Joanne Tomkins, *Post-colonial Drama: Theory, Practice, Politics*. London: Routledge, 1994. 137. Print.

Dover, Cedric. "The Black Knight." *Phylon (1940–1956)* 15. 2 (1964): 115–19. Print.

Du Bois, W. E. B. "Paying for Plays." *Crisis* 25 (December 1922): 7. Print.

———. *The Souls of Black Folk*. Chicago: A. C. McClurg & Co., 1903. Print.

Fanon, Franz. *The Wretched of the Earth*. Trans. Constance Farrington. New York: Grove, 1963. Print.

Finnegan, Ruth. *Oral Literature in Africa*. Oxford: Oxford UP, 1970. Print.

Gayle, Addison. *The Black Aesthetic*. New York: Doubleday, 1972. Print.

Gilbert, Helen, and Joanne Tompkins. *Post-colonial Drama: Theory, Practice, Politics*. London: Routledge, 1996. Print.

Glissant, Edouard. *Caribbean Discourses. Selected Essays*. Trans. Michael Dash. Charlottesville: UP of Virginia, 1999. Print.

Gomez, Michael. *Reversing the Sail: A History of the African Diaspora*. Cambridge: Cambridge UP, 2005. Print.

Harrison, Paul Carter. *The Drama of Nommo*. New York: Grove Press, 1972. Print.

Harrison, Paul Carter, Victor Leo Walker II, and Gus Edwards, eds. *Black Theatre: Ritual Performance in the African Diaspora*. Philadelphia: Temple UP, 2002. Print.

Hatch, James. "Some African Influences on the Afro-American Theatre." *The Theatre of Black Americans*. Ed. Errol Hill. New York: Applause Theatre and Cinema Books, 1980, 1987. 13–29. Print.

Hatch, James V., and Errol G. Hill. *A History of African American Theatre.* Cambridge Studies in American Theatre and Drama. Cambridge: Cambridge UP, 2003. Print.

Hunter, Margaret. *Race, Gender, and the Politics of Skin Tone.* New York: Routledge, 2005. Print.

Jeiyifo, Biodun. "The Reinvention of Theatrical Tradition." *Modern African Drama.* Norton Critical Edition. Ed. Biodun Jeyifo. New York: W.W. Norton, 2002. Print.

———, ed. *Modern African Drama.* Norton Critical Edition. New York: W.W. Norton, 2002. Print.

Jules-Rosette, Bennetta. *Black Paris: The African Writers' Landscape.* Foreword by Simon Njami. Chicago: U of Illinois P, 1998.

Lhamon, W. T., Jr. "Optic Black: Naturalizing the Refusal to Fit." *Black Cultural Traffic: Crossroads in Global Performance and Popular Culture.* Ed. Harry J. Elam Jr. and Kennell Jackson. Ann Arbor: U of Michigan P, 2008. 111–40. Print.

Locke, Alain, and Gregory Montgomery, eds. *Plays of Negro Life: A Source Book of Native American Drama.* Decorations and illustrations by Douglas Aaron. New York: Harper and Brothers, 1969. Print.

McKay, Claude. *A Long Way from Home.* Fort Washington, PA: Harvest Books, 1970. Print.

Mercer, Kobena. "Diaspora Aesthetics and Visual Culture." *Black Cultural Traffic: Crossroads in Global Performance and Popular Culture.* Ed. Harry J. Elam Jr. and Kennell Jackson. Ann Arbor: U of Michigan P, 2008. 141–61. Print.

Mullen, Harryette. "Optik White: Blackness and the Production of Whiteness." *Diacritics* 24 (Summer/Fall 1994): 711–89. Print.

Neale, Larry. "The Black Arts Movement." *The Black American Writer.* Vol. 2, *Poetry and Drama.* Ed. C. W. E. Bigsby. First published by Everett/Edward. Baltimore, MD: Pelican Books, 1969, 1971. 187–202. Print.

Ngugi wa Thiong'O. *Penpoints, Gunpoints, and Dreams: Towards a Critical Theory of the Arts and the State in Africa.* Oxford: Clarendon, 1998. Print.

Niane, D. T., Trans. *Sundiata: An Epic of Old Mali.* Harlow, UK: Longman, 1960, 1994. Print.

Okpewho, Isidore. *The Epic in Africa: Toward a Poetics of the Oral Performance.* New York: Columbia UP, 1979. Print.

———. *Myth in Africa: A Study of Its Aesthetics and Cultural Relevance.* Cambridge: Cambridge UP, 1983. Print.

Oliver, Roland, and Anthony Atmore. *Medieval Africa: 1250–1800.* Cambridge: Cambridge UP, 2001. Print.

Peterson, Bernard L. *Early Black American Playwrights and Dramatic Writers: A Biographical Directory and Catalog of Plays, Films, and Broadcasting Scripts.* Westport, CT: Greenwood, 1990. Print.

Richardson, Willis, ed. *The Black Horseman: Plays and Pageants from the Life of the Negro.* Jackson: UP of Mississippi, 1993. Print.

Richardson, Willis, and May Miller, eds. *Negro History in Thirteen Plays.* New York: Associated Publishers, 1935. Print.

Rubin, Don. "African Theatre in a Global Context." *Modern African Drama.* Norton Critical Edition. Ed. Biodun Jeyifo. New York: W.W. Norton, 2002. 410. Print.

Russell, Kathy, Midge Wilson, and Ronald Hall. *The Color Complex: The Politics of Skin Color among African Americans.* New York: Doubleday, 1993. Print.

Seshadri-Crooks, Kalana. *Desiring Whiteness: A Lacanian Analysis of Race.* London: Routledge, 2000. Print.

Slemon, Stephen. "Reading for Resistance." *A Shaping of Connections: Commonwealth Literature Studies Then and Now.* Ed. H. Maes-Jelinek, K. H. Petersen, and A. Rutherford. Sydney: Dangaroo, 1989. 100–15. Print.

Soyinka, Wole. *Art, Dialogue and Outrage: Essays on Literature and Culture.* Ibadan, Nigeria: New Horn, 1988. 134–46. Print.

———. *Myth, Literature, and the African World.* Cambridge: Cambridge UP, 1976. Print.

Spellman, A. B. "Big Bushy Afros." *International Review of African American Art* 15.1 (1998): 53. Print.

Spillers, Hortense. *Black, White, and in Color: Essays on American Literature and Culture.* Chicago: U of Chicago P, 2003. Print.

Stoval, Tyler. "Black Community, Black Spectacles: Performance and Race in Transatlantic Perspective." *Black Cultural Traffic: Crossroads in Global Performance and Popular Culture.* Ed. Harry J. Elam Jr. and Kennell Jackson. Ann Arbor: U of Michigan P, 2008. 221–41. Print.

Toure, Sekou Ahmed. Keynote address at the Congress of Black Writers and Artists held in Rome in 1959. Quoted in Franz Fanon, *The Wretched of the Earth.* Trans. by Constance Farrington. New York: Grove, 1959. Print.

Walcott, Derek. *Dream on Monkey Mountain. Dream on Monkey Mountain and Other Plays.* New York: Farrar, Straus and Giroux, 1970. 107–326. Print.

———. "What the Twilight Says: An Overture." *Dream on Monkey Mountain and Other Plays.* New York: Farrar, Straus and Giroux, 1970. 3–40. Print.

Wilson, August. "The Ground on which I Stand." *Callaloo* 20.3 (1998): 493–503. Print.

Wilson-Tagoe, Nana. "From Myth to Dialectic: History in Derek Walcott's Drama." *Historical Thought in West Indian Literature.* Miama: UP of Florida, 1998. 169–81. Print.

W. G. G. Review. "Plays and Pageants from the Life of the Negro." *Journal of Negro History* 15.2 (April 1930): 263–64. Print.

White, Hayden. *Metahistory: The Historical Imagination in Nineteenth-Century Europe.* Baltimore: The Johns Hopkins UP, 1973. Print.

2

THE ÒRÌṢÀ PARADIGM

An Overview of African-Derived Mythology, Folklore,
and Kinesthetic Dance Performatives

Benita Brown

[O]ur attitude towards the dance must change. We must cease to regard it as merely a conventionalized form of sex-expression, as the
tired business person's amusement, or as an intellectual and geometri-
cal problem unfolded to us at the concert hall. Dance may be all these,
but it is something more than these. Dance is a symbol of life—rhythmic, glorious, immortal. It is a language and a hieroglyphic of divinity.
Let us learn to speak it and to read it. (St. Denis and Miller 18)

The Òrìṣà Paradigm is a qualitative assessment examining the kinesthetic dance movements as well as the mythology and folklore of the gods
and goddesses (known as Òrìṣà) within the Yoruba pantheon. Yoruba
spiritual and cultural dance performatives are found throughout the
African Diaspora practiced by African Americans (and others) seeking to
re/connect with their African ancestry. As an African American, I have
practiced and performed African-derived dances onstage professionally
and socially, as well as during spiritual and communal ceremonies. Thus,
I utilize the tools of researcher/scholar, insider/outsider, and participant/
observer to identify, describe, and compare these African-derived dance
performatives as an African and African American cultural phenomenon
that continues in the twenty-first century.[1]

Theoretically, the Òrìṣà Paradigm (1) provides a descriptive and comparative analyses of African-derived spiritual, ecstatic, and cosmic dance forms and African American vernacular jazz dance performance; (2) analyzes, as an exemplar text, an African/African American cultural modality that defers and transfers African-derived mythology and folklore through nonverbal text; (3) recognizes the un/conscious manifestation of the Òrìṣà in the initiated/uninitiated "black dancing body";[2] and (4) postulates scholarly discourse about the presence of African-derived mythology and African American vernacular/jazz dance performatives.

Over the years, Afrocentric scholars have developed reflective discourse about African-derived vernacular/jazz dance as performed by African Americans.[3] These African-derived vernacular dance modalities are the foundation of the euphoric soul force and dancing spirit found within the African Diaspora: when analyzing African American vernacular/jazz dance culture, this phenomenon comes in the shape of nonsecular, secular, political, and sociocultural activities that bring into action ecstatic dancing. These dance performatives also help participants find ways of coping with life's circumstances as a result of enslavement as experienced by African Americans. Consider the following from Okagbue: "It is probably right to say that every person of African descent in the world today must have, directly or vicariously, participated in or experienced the psychic dislocation which both trans-Atlantic slavery and African colonization had brought about" (19).

Speaking of African Americans, DeFrantz posits that, "Black social dances contain dual transcripts of 'public' and 'private' meaning. These transcripts mirror constructions of outwardly entertaining and secretly derisive rhetoric articulated by black cultural theorists" (65). DeFrantz's statement is based upon the historical perspective of Du Bois (5), who contends that:

> After the Egyptian and Indian, the Greek and Roman, the Teuton and Mongolian, the Negro is a sort of seventh son, born with a veil, and gifted with second-sight in this American world,—world which yields him no true self-consciousness but only lets him see himself through the revelation of the other world. . . . One ever feels his twoness,—an American, A Negro; two souls, two thoughts, two unreconciled strivings; two warring ideals in one dark body, whose dogged strength alone keeps it from being torn asunder. . . . [The American Negro]

would not bleach his Negro soul in a flood of white Americanisms, for
he knows that Negro blood has a message for the world.

Accordingly, DeFrantz (64) juxtaposes Du Bois's "theory of double consciousness" with the Black dancing body and Black social dance, asserting that "double consciousness is a doubling of desire contained by the
tenacity of the black body released through dance." DeFrantz's insight
could be expanded to include that this "double consciousness," "tenacity," and "release" in dance is the groundwork for understanding the dual
relationship between dance as a social event and dance as a cosmic party
for the gods. African-derived cosmic, and ultimately ecstatic, dances may
well be the nonverbal "secretly derisive rhetoric" that is codified so that
only the insiders (participants and observers) would completely understand (un/consciously) that there are African-derived mythological and
folkloric symbolisms that undergird the foundation of an African
American vernacular jazz dance culture. This may well be the apparition
of an African past, the element of the double consciousness that exposes
and then transcends the spiritual threshold and presentation of the reincar-
nated kinesthetic dance movements of the Òrìṣà and their African-derived cultural milieu. Thus, African American vernacular dance culture
maintains a double meaning. It is a social event, but it is also sacred as it
uplifts the spirit and satisfies the soul of both practitioner and observer.
Concomitantly, it may well serve as supplication to the deities as well as
protest by the deities. For instance, Robert Hinton (4) notes that:

> Early in the slavery experience, Afro-American dance split into two
> basic streams. The first stream was the dance that Black folk created
> for themselves during those few precious hours of sacred and secular
> celebration. . . . The first stream was more "African" in part because of
> the movement quality and vocabulary. . . . The second stream was the
> dance that black people created for white people.

Hinton describes the secondary dance as the dance that was performed
under "duress" in order to appease a white audience. He further postulates
that the dance of celebration (including the sacred and secular) has become a "cross-fertilization and secularization into America's popular
dance—from the Ring Shout through Charleston, Jitterbug, and Disco, to
today's hardcore dancing" (4). Accordingly, one could look at African
American vernacular jazz dance performance and the African American

dancing body itself as embodiments of sociocultural and sacred behavior. In other words, the African American dancing body and performative becomes the human connection with African-derived mythological and folkloric deities such as the *Òrìṣà* from the Yoruba pantheon. Hence, Lincoln and Mamiya (7) posit:

> The core values of black culture like freedom, justice, equality, and African heritage, and racial parity at all levels of human intercourse, are raised to ultimate levels and legitimated by the black sacred cosmos. . . . The close relationship between the black sacred cosmos and black culture has often been missed by social analysts who impose sacred/secular distinctions too easily upon the phenomena of black culture.

African-derived kinesthetic dance forms are prevalent in the cultural structure of movement and music, and it is consistent with the ways that African Americans perform dance. At the un/conscious level, ecstatic dancing is at the core of the dance performatives, whether at a social event or sacred gathering, because the sacred and the secular are not separate when it comes to African American vernacular dance practices. This position is validated by Dixon-Gottschild (280), who writes:

> And let us not forget the basic praise dance that is still the most prevalent. It has no name—not even Ring Shout—but it is created, case by case, by the dancing bodies of individuals who are inspired by and enthralled in the Holy Spirit and simply get up and dance as the spirit moves them. Then and now, and in a multitude of ways, people of African lineage continue dancing the spirit.

THE ÒRÌṢÀ OF YORUBA LAND

The *Òrìṣà* are the protagonists of cultural practices and belief systems in Nigeria, Benin, Togo, and Ghana.[4] The creators of one of the richest cultural traditions in Africa, the Yoruba people lived in this area since antiquity. They were the rulers of the Ife Kingdom (twelfth century) and Oyo Kingdom (sixteenth to nineteen centuries). During the eighteenth century, millions of Yoruba were captured and sold as slaves. Even though they were under the oppressive lash of enslavement, members of the Yoruba ethnic group continued their spiritual inclinations under the pretext of belief systems conceptualized by Catholicism, Protestant Christianity, Native American mythology, and Kardecan spiritism. Consequently, the Yoruba pantheon became infused within New World religious practices. Although clandestine in their cultural rituals and practices, participants of the Yoruba belief systems have a significant following throughout the Americas with scattered practices throughout the Western hemisphere. The Yoruba *Odu Ifa* (sacred scripture) has been passed down through oral traditions and syncretized with various religions in North, Central, and South America as well as Europe and Asia.[5]

Yoruba mythology contains anecdotes describing how the *Òrìṣà* became identified by their particular human attributes and supernatural feats. Mythology and folklore consistently repeat the anecdotes belonging to the divine spirits as they once lived on earth as human beings and earned historical significance as kings and queens, as well as high priests and priestesses. They maintained exceptional accomplishments and implemented major communal contributions. The *Òrìṣà* are idiosyncratic: their names and functions vary based on geographical locations, codified languages, psychological affiliations, social and cultural practices, work patterns, and environmental influences.

According to Yoruba mythology, Olodumare, the Supreme Being, is the creator of heaven and earth along with a multitude of spiritual deities and ancestral spirits. At any given geographical location, there can be anywhere from 1,000 to 4,000 minor deities and 401 major deities within the Yoruba pantheon, with a special inclination toward 16 deities as practiced in Nigeria and North America, for example. Olodumare is not worshipped directly by human beings but approached by virtue of the wishes and instructions of deities and ancestors through divination and prayer. Mythology, folklore, music, ritual, ecstatic dance, codified language, folk arts, material culture, and sacrifices are allegorically used to communicate, adhere, invoke, appease, and confer thanks for blessings received from Olodumare.

Ritual activity involving dance is a shared phenomenon among most of humanity. Sociocultural practices that respond to the environment, including elements of political inclinations, time and space, rhythmical structure, material culture, foodstuffs, music, and kinesthetic dance movements can be found among many cultures throughout the world. What is different about African-derived, African American vernacular/

jazz dance performatives is the ritualizing (or preparation) for the dance as both sacred and secular events that encourage and accompany ecstatic dancing. Further, the music dictates the dance movements as the dance is the nonverbal un/conscious communication with the Òrìṣà. In traditional West African dance performatives such as those performed by the Yoruba's embracing of the Òrìṣà, there is no separation between the dance and the music. The same phenomenon appears in early jazz where, for instance, the dance and music are both referred to as jazz. The music provides impetus for the dance, and the dancer is very careful to stay within the rhythmic structure of the music until there occurs what is known in vernacular terms as the "breakaway." It is from the "breakaway" that the dancer transitions into improvisation or impromptu dance movements that usher in what appears to be euphoria and/or spiritual possession. This type of behavior can be witnessed among dancers, musicians, and singers and is sometimes shared with observers who would signify that mutual experience by vocalizing indiscernible hollers. Writing about the participatory nature of African art and culture, Gyekye observes that,

> Art in traditional African cultures has both functional and purely aesthetic dimensions. One outstanding feature of artistic performances such as music and dance is their participatory character: music-making and dancing are communal activities, aimed—apart from their purely aesthetic qualities—at deepening communal sentiments and consciousness. Among the criteria of aesthetic value and judgment are appropriateness and fittingness. Music, dancing, and even clothing must be appropriate to the occasion. Beauty is seen not only in works of art and in the human figure but also in human conduct, in humanity itself, and in a person's character. (178)

Whether it is a secular activity such as hand-dancing at the club on Saturday night or a religious experience such as receiving the Holy Ghost during Sunday morning church services, there remains evidence of African-derived kinesthetic dance performatives that also maintain ritualized activities and ecstatic dancing. These sociocultural functions keep African-derived mythology, folklore, ritual, ecstatic dance, foodstuffs, and material culture enlivened through the practices of people of African descent who, at an un/conscious level, continue with the ritual and folkloric activities emanating from the African cultural continuum. The evidence is strong when it comes to African American vernacular jazz dance performative: the characteristics, modalities, and kinesthetic dance movements of the *Òrìṣà* appear to happen at both conscious and unconscious levels, with the unconscious level being specifically true for the uninitiated.

According to Àjàyí (45), "Without a regular communication systems ensured through the rituals of worship, the gods become irrelevant and cease to exist in the people's consciousness and reality." Furthermore, she contends that:

> Rituals are constantly recurring performances with prescribed forms and constitute a people's attempt to legitimize and perpetuate their dominate conceptual values. . . . Thus, rituals, in addition to being significant pointers to how a people think about themselves, have built-in structures to cope with new crises and to initiate and create new concepts thereof. This "self-generative" quality further enriches the form and content of the ritualized content. (46)

Thus, it is through the invisible, unknown, and graininess of this "self-generative" process, experienced in time and space by the dancer, that the ancestors and deities are escorted into the human realm. In this process they equally manifest their powers through the medium of the dancer.

As I have already indicated, *Òrìṣà* worship in the African Diaspora embraces the tenets of African-derived mythology and folklore originating from the Yoruba pantheon. Hence, spiritual activities are perpetuated through rituals by and for those who are devotees. Initiates adhere to very strict protocols under the supervision of priests and priestesses who are leaders of worship and keepers of the tenets found within the pantheon. However, when considering the African-derived cultural modality within the context of African American kinesthetic and vernacular/jazz dance performatives, the practice of the *Òrìṣà*'s performatives juxtapose dance performatives within the sacred and nonsacred as practiced at the un/conscious level. This phenomenon is where we find the implementation of ecstatic dance. The dancers may or may not be initiated devotees, but their performative characteristics are reminiscent of kinesthetic dance movements that originate with African-derived dance movements and the cultural modalities that accompany the dance. As one may witness at a worship ceremony, dancers incorporate improvisational dance movements that evoke euphoric and supernatural behavior.[6] Àjàyí (221) posits that,

> Dance makes and becomes art in the way it unifies external tangible elements such as movement, rhythm, and space in the body to create a new cohesive form. This new form, the dance, becomes a powerful non-verbal communication symbol. This is because the body in its dual role as the primary tool of dance and a cultural indicator is the tangible element able to turn cultural concepts into perceptible forms narrated in rhythmic movement and contextualized in space.

Also, with regard to Africa-derived performatives among African Americans, Jonathan Jackson (44) argues that, "In black vernacular dancing, improvisation means the creative structuring, or choreographing, of human movement in the moment of ritual performance." For her part, Daniel (353) provides the following perspective:

> In the dance practices of Yoruba/Lucumi/Santeria, the physical body becomes the social body, both the repository of knowledge from the collective memory of a variety of African ethnic groups, and the sensitized reactor of modern transnational culture. The body is dressed in memory and spiritual clothing while in performance; it drinks of archaic chants and ancient rhythms as well as from synthesized and electronic sound concoctions.

Daniel (356) goes on to note that,

> Dancing keeps us healthy, sane, balanced, strong, vital, vivacious, continually growing! It does so by enlivening and continually revitalizing the transformational process of living. The concrete act of dancing affords the immediacy of both the learned and intuitive realms of knowledge, and empowers humans as well as transforms and identifies them with and as spiritual entities.

KINESTHETIC DANCE MOVEMENTS OF THE ÒRÌṢÀ

There are seven major/legendary deities from the Yoruba pantheon that have maintained their presence in the lives of Yoruba devotees. Among devotees in the United States, they are frequently called the Seven

African Powers, and they each have their particular aspects of ruling over the forces of nature, the cosmos, and humanity. The same attributes are found throughout African-derived mythology and folklore with various levels of modification, syncretism, and diversity at various geographic locations, especially where African enslavement was predominant. The major deities worshipped throughout the United States are (1) Èṣù, Òrìṣà of the crossroads, doorways, and gates; (2) Ṣàngó, Òrìṣà of thunder, lightning, dance, and passion; (3) Ọbàtàlá, Òrìṣà of the white cloth who rules over the mind, intellect, and cosmic equilibrium; (4) Yemoja, Òrìṣà of the ocean and the moon, guardian of childbirth and fertility, who also rules the subconscious and creative endeavors; (5) Òsun, Òrìṣà of love, passion, sensuality, money, and prosperity; (6) Ògún, Òrìṣà of war, blood, and iron, and chief of warriors; and (7) Ọya, Òrìṣà over storms, lightning, transformation, and change.

The following analysis draws on only three of the Òrìṣà (Ṣàngó, Ọya, and Òsun) as a way to describe the characteristics and presence in African-derived mythology, folklore, and kinesthetic, vernacular/jazz

Figure 2.1.   The Kulu Mele African Dance and Drum Ensemble of Philadelphia performing Ọbàtàlá (the Òrìṣà of the white cloth) in Nigerian-styled costumes. Photo by Jaci Downs.

dance performatives as practiced in the United States of America. When observing the kinesthetic dance movements, preferences, and characteristics of Ṣàngó, for example, the dancer leans forward with knees bent while one foot is raised in the air. In this position, the deity begins to possess and mount the devotee who then performs a stamping movement with emphasis on the downbeat, which is immediately followed by a disyllabic foot pattern within a count of a six/eight measure of music. In Cuba, Ṣàngó's style of dance is performed by circular movements of the pelvic area as a demonstration of the male prowess that is characteristic of this deity. Similar foot patterns are found in African-derived vernacular/jazz dance movements such as the Philly bop, where the emphasized movement of the pelvic area is performed mostly by males.[7] These foot patterns and pelvic movements are also performed in soul line dancing.[8] The dance performatives of Ọya (one of Ṣàngó's wives) are represented by the turning and twirling of the wind. Daniel (354) speaks of Ọya's characteristics and dance patterns: "she whirls, spins, and churns like the tornadoes, hurricanes, and cyclones. Her spinning force connotes that she has little fear of others, of death, or even of fear itself; she is female all powerful."

The dance performatives of Òsun (another of Ṣàngó's wives) are similar to bop movements performed by both female and male dancers without the emphasis of the foot-stamping patterns. Òsun's characteristics are that of the flirtatious, coquettish goddess of beauty, love, and wealth. Òsun's kinesthetic dance movements, coming from Cuba, are subtle while flirtatious, and she uses the swaying motion of her hips from right to left, emphasizing the pelvic area while using coquettish behavior, as her mating tool. These kinesthetic dance movements that focus on the pelvic area are mainly seen in couple dances such as the slow drag and two-step. These movements can also be seen in African American shake dances as well as hip-hop dance movements.

Both Ọya's and Òsun's movements described above are similar to the performatives of the African American vernacular/jazz dance movements generally known as the bop but also known as the swing, jitterbug, handdancing, and more. The names of these dances vary from one geographical region in the United States to the other; however, all contain the same rhythmic foot patterns found in African-derived kinesthetic, vernacular/jazz dance movements. The dancers execute general foot patterns as well as implement variations that arise due to the improvisational nature of the performance. Nonetheless, even when they are performing improvisational movements, which are in most cases very similar to African-derived dances, the dancers stay within the structure of the rhythmic foot pattern.

The following is a basic description of the dance as observed by the author in North Philadelphia (United States) during the 1960s.[9] The bop starts out with a couple holding hands and facing each other with right foot forward. The left foot is behind the front foot in a position mirrored by each partner. First, they establish their timing by doing the basic step, a duple, beginning with the right, front foot and leaning forward with knees bent. This is immediately followed by a duple on the left foot. When the left foot is working, the dancers lean back onto it, and when the right foot is used, the dancers lean forward while holding each other's hands and inclining the hands toward the floor. After the initial left-right duple, the dancers open up by taking the right foot and sliding it behind the left foot, emphasizing the right foot to a count of one beat, immediately followed by another count on the left foot. The dancers' positions at this point are opened up away from each other, but they are still holding each other's right hand in the front while the left hand is wrapped around the other's waist. They return to the initial step pattern once again to establish the basic pattern before the variations of the step pattern for the bop are reestablished. Afterward, the male dancer sends the female dancer out in a movement that is sometimes called the break or breakaway. During the breakaway the left hand is free while each partner continues to hold the other's right hand. It is at this point that African-derived improvisational movements are performed by the dancers and differential styles are exhibited. The male and female dancers connect with each other's movement pattern within the framework of the improvisation, simultaneously keeping in time with the basic duple/duple and single/single steps. This ensures that when they return to holding each other by the waist, the transition is smooth and uninterrupted, facilitating the ease with which the basic bop step is reestablished. This goes on throughout the duration of the music, and the improvised movements are executed according to rhythmic timing. In a 1994 interview with John W. Roberts, Jennifer McMichael offers the following observation regarding both the in-step and improvisational elements of the bop.

> [The bop] became a popular dance because it showed style even with a partner. You could dance the "bop" with a partner, holding hands, and

something like jitterbugging. But a lot of times when you "jitter-bugged" or "boogie-woogied" you did the same things. When you dance and spin your partner out you both did the same steps. . . . In the "bop" you are supposed to follow a sequence of dancing, but each time there was a variation where the man would hold his pants, pull up his pants leg [and] show his shoes off. And when he showed his shoes off he would twist his foot like this while he's dancing. . . . Now a woman wouldn't do that, but what she would do was . . . she would put her hand behind the back of her [crinoline skirt] and while she's doing that would swing her dress out, and the dress would flare.

Evident in McMichael's description of the bop are performatives equally belonging to Ṣàngó, Ọya, and Òsun. This can be seen in the movement of the male dancer who she describes as showing off by pulling his trouser leg up, an example of Ṣàngó's performative, and spinning the female dancer around to evidence Ọya's performative. Equally, by swinging her dress out so that her dress would flare, the female dancer is able to signal performatives belonging to Òsun. These dance performatives originate primarily in Cuba, with its strong connection to the African-derived dance movements of the *Òrìṣà*, and have been (re)created in the United States.

ÒRÌṢÀ PARADIGM AND TRANSFORMATIVE PERFORMANCE

As mentioned earlier, during the improvisational movements, dancers conjure up their own movement style and foot patterns but stay in the basic rhythmic structure of the accompanying music. Some dancers appear to experience euphoria as they carve out their personal movement expressions while out on the dance floor. When dancers are really showing off their skills, this solicits emotive responses from observers. Highly skilled dancers draw a crowd that encircles them as they continue to perform. The euphoria becomes contagious, and participants and observers seem to enter an emotional realm that passes through a spiritual threshold as they enter into a euphoric experience. Thus, the *Òrìṣà* Paradigm claims that ritualizing the African-derived dance performatives (to include and/or bring about ecstatic dancing), cultural practices, mythological characters, and folkloric practices accompanied by music, song, and

drama significantly assist the individual's ability to open himself or herself up to the spiritual realm: that is the goal, and it is purposeful. Dance
is a communicative phenomenon that creates a spiritual connection and
permeates the well-being of the society as a whole. As Àjàyí (224) states:

> By serving as the receptacle for other art forms, dance heightens and
> enhances their as well as its own significance, communication and
> aesthetic value. This quality is most vividly demonstrated in Yoruba
> religious context where dance functions effectively as the language
> that bridges the chasm of communication between transcendental cos-
> mic powers and human beings.

"KRUMPING"

Although this chapter has used early African American vernacular jazz
dance performatives as well as vernacular dance performances in Philadelphia as examples of African-derived mythology and folklore in dance,
other dances fit the mold. The heading of this section is from the film
Rize directed by Dave LaChapelle (2005).

This film is an important documentary/drama that contains firsthand
evidence of the presence of African-derived mythology, folklore, and
African American kinesthetic dance performatives within a style of urban
dancing called krumping. This style of dance is very similar to the kinesthetic movements of African-derived ritual dances. For example, in one
scene a young woman appears after an exuberant krumping performance.
She exhibits behavior associated with possession during which she rejoices and speaks in audible yelps. Afterward she is physically unable to
walk and so is literally carried away. The camera zooms in on a young
man who speaks directly into the lens, saying, "she got struck [and] that's
what we waited for." In a different scene, another young man is flailing
his arms and his facial expression is otherworldly; his eyes are wide open
but he seems to be looking far beyond what is right in front of him. As he
dances vivaciously, people gather around him. They let him continue
with the dance but take precautions to make sure he doesn't hurt himself.

For the female dancer in the film, the characteristics and behavior are
very similar to the mounting and possession of a devotee belonging to
O̩ya because of her verbalized but indistinct murmurs of rejoicing. On the
other hand, the young man's flailing arms and facial expressions are

similar to the mounting and possession of a devotee of Ṣàngó. Here, the hypothesis of the Òrìṣà Paradigm takes credence; that is, the un/conscious adherence to African-derived mythology and folklore is evident in African-derived kinesthetic vernacular/jazz dance performatives. Even though it is beyond the scope of this chapter, the Òrìṣà Paradigm may possibly be considered as an acceptable model when speaking about African-derived kinesthetic, vernacular/jazz dance performatives.

CONCLUSION

The Òrìṣà Paradigm encapsulates the various undergirding of African-derived spiritual belief systems and ancestral deference at the subliminal level, encompassing epic memory, sociocultural practices, and performative kinesthetic dance movements. Providing a descriptive analysis of the cultural milieu derived from Africa as practiced in the Diaspora is quite a challenge because African derivations are multifaceted, multicolored, polycentric, and curvilinear, geographically inclined, broad-based, and ever changing. Mythological, folkloric, kinesthetic qualities and creative performances of the many African ethnicities and their offspring maintain their behavioral foundations of sacred activities that are intrinsically based upon their African-derived spirituality. Through their cultural practices and emotions, they seek the approval and presence of the African-derived deities and ancestors in their myriad manifestations. Thus, the Òrìṣà Paradigm places religious, philosophic, cultural, sacred, and sociocultural practices at the center of analyzing African-derived mythology and folklore and its accompanying kinesthetic dance performatives. Philosophical and religious scholars have asserted the multifaceted presence of the Holy Spirit in African-based cultures. According to Mbiti, the Most High embodies nature, the cosmos, animate and inanimate objects, the universe, the ancestors, celestial beings, and human beings.[10] For his part, Molette (9) observes that, "The Afro-American aesthetic places a very high value upon emotionally motivated behavior; or another term might be used to describe it would be spiritually motivated behavior."

It is important to acknowledge the connection between soul and spirit as an important facilitator of dance because the dancer executes movements that promote emotive responses from the participants and observers, and this serves to uplift the spirit and soul of society. Thus, the presence of soul and the possession of the spirit uplift and possibly unify the community. This sort of connection helps both observers and participants to confirm the community's innermost feelings because the dancer is a vehicle to the spiritual world. She or he unites the community with the Most High through devotion to the deities as expressed through music, song, drama, and, especially, African-derived dance movements. These media are the components of the African American kinesthetic, vernacular/jazz dance performatives, which, in my view, support the premise of the Òrìṣà Paradigm.

NOTES

Continuing the premise upon which I wrote my doctoral thesis while completing graduate studies at Temple University's Dance Department in 1999, I have used the title Òrìṣà Paradigm as an envelope of scholarship that tells my own story in my own words. This idea is corroborated by Sheila Walker's discourse on W. E. B. Du Bois (24). Walker contends that, "We are insisting upon seeing and portraying ourselves through the revelations of our own experiences and interpretations, as opposed to through the revelations of others based on their experiences and interpretations that are usually different from and sometimes antithetical to our own." While the Òrìṣà are the closest to me insofar as my personal spiritual preferences are concerned, they are also representative of belief systems of African Americans from those who practice within the pantheon of the Akan to those who worship the pantheon of Ausar/Auset. Traditional African religions (overall) have a plethora of deities, lesser deities, as well as ancestral practices that are (for the most part) the same but different. In addition, my use of North Philadelphia (1960s) as the exemplar text in no way negates the exemplary cultural phenomenon in dance performance that has occurred throughout the African Diaspora, inclusive of those of us who live in the United States of America.

1. My use of the term "performative" relates to the action and interaction, the role of spectator and observer, the energy of the dance and the dancer, the culture and the relevant mythology/folklore, the environment and sociocultural practices that accompany the dance. These are what I consider as the performatives of the dance. Thus, while this chapter is a descriptive analysis that includes my experience as a North Philadelphia (United States) dancer and its (North Philadelphia) particular style of dance (especially insofar as the Philly bop and the Philly cha-cha is concerned), in no way do I present these as the ultimate and only dance experience among those of the African Diaspora. As the term Òrìṣà Paradigm is used as an exemplar text, so is the term "Philly bop" where it is used as an example to point out the continuous mythology and folklore that is present within African American vernacular dance culture.

2. See Brenda Dixon-Gottschild, The Black Dancing Body: A Geography from Coon to Cool (New York: Palgrave MacMillan, 2003).

3. When I refer to the Afrocentric model, I am referring to Africa as a central reference in discourse about African and African-derived culture, specifically in

reference to dance. Some scholars use other terms to describe African cultural retentions. For example, terms such as Africanist (Brenda Dixon-Gottschild) and Afrogenic (Sheila Walker) have been used to describe cultural retentions in the African Diaspora. In reference to dance, some use Black Dance (Jonathan Jackson) or Black Dancing Body (Brenda Dixon-Gottschild, Thomas F. DeFrantz). I believe they are all appropriate and the authors have the freedom to use their own terminology. I use the term Afrocentric to describe and place African culture throughout the Diaspora as the center of discourse in my conversations about Africa and African-derived dance. This is the fruit of my own personal exposure to the teachings of Molefi Kete Asante and Kariamu Welsh.

4. Although scholars often view African spiritual activities as "religious practices," for the purposes of this chapter I borrow from Kwame Gyekye's position in *African Cultural Values: An Introduction* (4) where he argues that "in African life and thought, the religious is not distinguished from the nonreligious, the sacred from the secular, the spiritual from the material."

5. See Yosef A. A. Ben-Jochannan, *African Origins of the Major Western Religions* (Baltimore, MD: Black Classic Press, 1970). Also see M. A. De La Torre, *Santería: The Beliefs and Rituals of a Growing Religion in America* (Grand Rapids, MI: Wm. B. Eerdmans, 2004).

6. In prior writings, I have termed this phenomenon as a "shout" culture emanating from the sacred/secular dance(s) of the "ring shout." My recent research has led me to believe that further study of the ring shout, shout, ring dance, and the like deserves a treatise of its own. Whereas the ring shout was originally a sacred religious ceremony often practiced in secret by enslaved Africans after the slave owner's worship services, the question that comes to mind is who and what the Africans were worshipping. An understanding of traditional African religions reveals that among the many ethnicities in Africa, worship of the ancestors and deities with their accompanying folkloric and cultural patterns was the mainstay of African religious worship, and dance was the central to all worship ceremonies.

7. These foot patterns are also found in swing and stepping.

8. Soul line dancing is a recent dance phenomenon that has been popularized by African Americans in the North and somewhat in the South. It uses R&B, soul, jazz, and hip-hop music, and communities of dancers create the choreography that is performed in groups at social events.

9. In North Philadelphia (1960s), teenagers formed social clubs that were organized purely for dance. These dances (slow drag, bop, and strand) were used as a part of the mating process.

10. See John S. Mbiti's *Introduction to African Religion*, 2nd ed. (Portsmouth, NH: Heinemann Educational Publishers, 1991).

WORKS CITED

Àjàyí, Omofolabo S. *Yoruba Dance: The Semiotics of Movement and Body Attitude in a Nigerian Culture.* Trenton, NJ: Africa World, 1998. Print.

Asante, Molefi Kete, and Kariamu Asante-Welsh. *African Culture: The Rhythms of Unity.* Westport, CT: Greenwood, 1985. Print.

Asante, Molefi Kete, and Mark T. Mattson. *The Historical and Cultural Atlas of African Americans.* New York: Macmillan, 1991. Print.

Bell, Michael J. *The World from Brown's Lounge: An Ethnography of Black Middle-Class Play.* Urbana: U of Illinois P, 1983.

Ben-Jochannan, Yosef A. A. *African Origins of the Major Western Religions.* Baltimore, MD: Black Classic Press, 1970.

Brown, Benita Junette. "'Boppin' at Miss Mattie's Place": African-American Grassroots Dance Culture in North Philadelphia from the Speakeasy to the Uptown Theater during the 1960s. Diss. Temple University, 1999. Ann Arbor, MI: UMI Dissertation Services, 2000 (UMI no. 9956528). Print.

Brown, Benita Junette. Dannabang Kuwabong, and Christopher Olsen. *The Presence of African-Derived Mythology in Literature, Dance, and Drama.* Mason, OH: Cengage Learning, 2012.

Daniel, Yvonne. "Embodied Knowledge in African American Dance Performance." *African Roots/American Culture: Africa in the Creation of the Americas.* Lanham: Rowman & Littlefield, 2001. Print.

De La Torre, Miguel A. *Santeria: The Beliefs and Rituals of a Growing Religion in America.* Grand Rapids, MI: William B. Eerdmans, 2004. Print.

DeFrantz, Thomas F., ed. *Dancing Many Drums, Excavations in African American Dance.* Madison: U of Wisconsin P, 2001.

Dixon-Gottschild, Brenda. *The Black Dancing Body: A Geography from Coon to Cool.* New York: Palgrave Macmillan, 2003. Print.

Du Bois, W. E. B. *The Philadelphia Negro: A Social Study.* New York: Schocken, 1967. Reprint.

———. *The Souls of Black Folk: Essays and Sketches.* New York: Dodd, Mead, 1979. Print.

Emery, Lynne Fauley. *Black Dance: From 1619 to Today.* Princeton, NJ: Princeton Book, 1988. Print.

Friedland, L. "Disco: Afro-American Vernacular Performance." *Dance Research Journal* 15.2 (1983): 27–35. Print.

Gwaltney, J. L. *Drylongso: A Self-Portrait of Black America.* New York: New Press, 1993. Print.

Gyekye, Kwame. *African Cultural Values: An Introduction.* Philadelphia: Sankofa, 1996. Print.

Hansen, C. "Jenny's Toe: Negro Shaking Dances in America." *American Quarterly* 19.3 (1967): 554–63. Print.

Harley, Sharon. *The Timetables of African American History: A Chronology of the Most Important People and Events in African American History.* New York: Simon and Shuster, 1995. Print.

Hazzard-Donald, Katrina. *Jookin': The Rise of Social Dance Formations in African-American Culture.* Philadelphia: Temple UP, 1990. Print.

Hill, Errol G. *The Theater of Black Americans: A Collection of Critical Essays.* Vol. 2, *The Presenters: Companies of Players, The Participators: Audiences and Critics.* Englewood Cliffs, NJ: Prentice-Hall, 1980. Print.

Hinton, R. *The Black Tradition in American Modern Dance.* Durham, NC: American Dance Festival, 1988. Print.

The History of Black People in Philadelphia, Pennsylvania. Philadelphia: Council of Independent Black Institutions, 1975. Print.

Holloway, Joseph E., ed. *Africanisms in American Culture.* Bloomington: Indiana UP, 1990. Print.

Jackson, Jonathan. "Improvisation in African American Vernacular Dance." *Dance Research Journal* 33.2 (2001): 40–53. JSTOR. Web.

Jamison, Judith, and Howard Kaplan. *Dancing Spirit: An Autobiography*. New York: Doubleday, 1993. Print.

Lane, Roger. *Roots of Violence in Black Philadelphia, 1860–1900*. Cambridge, MA: Harvard UP, 1986. Print.

Lapsansky, E. J. *Before the Model City: A Historical Exploration of North Philadelphia*. Philadelphia: Physical Environment Task Force and Philadelphia Model Cities Program for the Philadelphia Historical Commission, 1968. Print.

Levine, Lawrence W. *Black Culture and Black Consciousness: Afro-American Folk Thought from Slavery to Freedom*. New York: Oxford UP, 1977. Print.

Lincoln, C. Eric, and Lawrence H. Mamiya. *The Black Church in the African-American Experience*. Durham, NC: Duke UP, 1990. Print.

Molette, C. "Afro-American Ritual Drama." *Black World* 22.6 (1973): 4–12. Print.

Murphy, Joseph M. *Working the Spirit: Ceremonies of the African Diaspora*. Boston: Beacon, 1994. Print.

Okagbue, Osy A. *Culture and Identity in African and Caribbean Theatre*. London: Adonis and Abbey, 2009. Print.

"Philly Bop * Cha-Cha * Strand * Basic Line Dance Class & Detroit Ballroom Lessons." Posted by ahb3027. Online video clip. *YouTube*. YouTube, 30 June 2009. Web. 13 Apr. 2013.

Preston-Dunlop, Valerie Monthland, and Ana Sanchez-Colberg. *Dance and the Performative: A Choreological Perspective; Laban and Beyond*. London: Verve, 2002. Print.

Rize. Dir. D. LaChapelle. Perf. Documentary. Lions Gate, 2005. DVD.

Roberts, John W., ed. *Odunde*. Philadelphia: S.n., 1980. Print.

Rogers, J. W. *Odunde: From Hucklebuck to Hip Hop: Social Dance in the African American Community in Philadelphia*. Philadelphia: DIANE, 1995. Print.

St. Denis, Ruth, and Kamae A. Miller. *Wisdom Comes Dancing: Selected Writings of Ruth St. Denis on Dance, Spirituality, and the Body*. Seattle, WA: PeaceWorks, 1997. Print.

Walker, Sheila S. *African Roots / American Cultures: Africa in the Creation of the Americas*. Lanham, MD: Rowman & Littlefield, 2001. Print.

3

PERFORMATIVE BODY LANGUAGE IN SUZAN-LORI PARKS'S *VENUS* AND LYNN NOTTAGE'S *RUINED*

African Female Bodies through African American Eyes

Christopher Olsen

Mythologizing historical figures in Africa often requires playwrights to use vivid images and larger-than-life portrayals of those individuals. When one thinks of the many plays written about Shaka Zulu and his bravery against overwhelming odds or the images of the assassinated President Lumumba of the Congo as a spiritual presence in contemporary African life, one realizes that the "great" figures of African history are customarily treated as symbols rather than complicated psychological characters. African leaders become symbols of physical or spiritual power, and storytellers recount the events and actions of these important figures in African history, not unlike the heroic poems from Homer and other Greek poets. However, when mythologizing African women, a different tack is often taken. African women have been turned into symbols of courage and fortitude as well (for instance, the many warrior queens, such as Nzingha from what is now Angola), but more often than not they are presented as victimized and exploited. Many scholars have written about the Black woman's body and how it turns into a metaphor for a patriarchal gaze. The body can represent sexuality, sensuality, war zones, conquest, domestication, and rape, among other signifiers. The vivid image of an African woman's body has been presented onstage, and playwrights have manipulated its semiotic nature, either in the context of exposing the hierarchical male gaze of the reader/audience or as a device to embolden and empower female superiority by using it as a symbol of female survival.

Suzan-Lori Parks and Lynn Nottage are African American playwrights who have both explored female bodies in their work and have both mythologized (and exposed the mythology of) African women, particularly with regard to the image of their bodies. In 1995 Parks wrote *Venus*, which brings the character of the Venus Hottentot to life and uses African storytelling techniques to tell her story. Nottage wrote *Ruined* in 2008; the play is based on interviews with Congolese women who survived the violence and destruction of two civil wars. Both playwrights use African female bodies as metaphors for the exploitation and mythologizing of African women.

The tragic phenomenon known as the Venus Hottentot has generated massive scholarly scrutiny over the last thirty years, particularly just prior to August 2002 when her remains were finally buried in the Gamtoos River Valley in the Eastern Cape of South Africa. Sara Baartman, a Khoikhoi woman, was working as a slave in Cape Town, South Africa, in 1810 when she was duped into coming to England by an English ship's doctor. She was promised money and freedom if she would agree to display herself as a scientific curiosity. This display of Baartman's body, exhibited as a kind of freak of nature, turned out to be a voyeuristic experience for British audiences ogling an African woman with large genitals and buttocks. The term Hottentot is a derogatory Dutch label for the Khoisan people and is no longer used. In the early 1800s, however, rampant racism combined with social Darwinism bolstered the European sense of superiority over Africans, and the Venus Hottentot, as she was ironically called, became a symbol for the marginalization of the Khoisan peoples. She was described as being displayed on a "stage two feet high, along which she was led by her keeper and exhibited like a wild beast, being obliged to walk, stand, or sit as ordered" (Chambers 621). The abolition of slavery in England had occurred only three years earlier, and the newly founded African Association campaigned against her demeaning treatment. Four years later she moved to Paris but continued to allow herself to be displayed at social functions. Her abuse took its toll, and she died of alcoholism and possibly syphilis in 1815. Napoleon's surgeon general, George Cuvier, claimed her body and then conducted an extensive anthropological study of it after her death, concluding she was evidence of the superiority of the white race. He took her remains and exhibited them in the Musée de l'Homme. It wasn't until the 1970s that complaints from South Africa and elsewhere about the macabre display caused French museum officials to remove it. It wasn't until 2002, however, that her remains were finally returned to her home soil.

So, why continue writing about this phenomenon? Well, for one thing, Sara Baartman's experience has inspired a wealth of literature studying ethnological displays of Africans in the nineteenth century, examining Black female sexuality, and chronicling sexual models for contemporary African American females. Sander Gilman's groundbreaking article on the iconography of female sexuality in the late nineteenth century points to a Victorian fascination with women's genitalia—particularly with oversized examples—which confirmed the belief that African women were more primitive than Europeans because their bodies were grotesque and overly sexual (219). Gilman makes a connection between the highly sexualized images of homegrown prostitutes and exotic African women, both of which were highly sexualized creatures in the nineteenth century who needed to be controlled by white patriarchal forces (237). Strother agrees with Gilman by examining the connection between Europeans' fascination with African female sexuality and the antierotic display of Sara Baartman. This contradictory dual perception that the Khoisan culture is savage on one hand but beautiful on the other reinforces the adage that male slaves were sexually threatening whereas female slaves were sexually reassuring (2). Hammond's article on Black female sexuality points to the resistance of African American scholars to more rigorously examining sexuality within their own community (94). She quotes one scholar, Hortense Spillers, who writes: "Black women are the beached whales of the sexual universe. Unvoiced, unseen, not doing, awaiting their verb" (92). Recently, Stephens and Phillips have helped fill this void with an examination of African American sexual models constrained to "Freaks, Golddiggers, Divas, and Dykes" (2003). They postulate that sexual scripts influence their relationship with peers, potential partners, and the broader society. Because women's bodies have always been objectified by men in art, and have often been fetishized as creatures with exotic and grotesque characteristics, the African American female "other" has had to endure a particularly tortuous journey from object to subject.

The exotic and grotesque of the "other" has been treated in theatre since the ancient Greeks and has enjoyed renewed currency in contemporary theatre. Sometimes the person is dramatized as literally grotesque with physical deformities or mental deviations. In such plays as *Kaspar*, *Joe Egg*, and *The Elephant Man*, however, the victims turn into sympathetic figures (usually because they are tortured men or sympathetic children) with admirable qualities. When the "other" is seen as an attractive and exotic woman, playwrights have created a more complicated framework. The Western male's perception of highly idealized women can be frequently seen in a Western male's "gaze" of Asian women. This perception/misperception can be vividly seen in such plays as David Henry Hwang's *M. Butterfly* and in such films as *The World of Suzi Wong*. African women, however, have escaped this literary treatment in part because of the effects of the era of glorified primitivism in the nineteenth century and the absence of intercultural stage models based on a deep-seated racism.

Suzan-Lori Parks, a very successful African American playwright, has had a rich career as a writer (and rewriter) of African American historical events and literally "alienates" her characters—deliberately putting them in positions of otherness. She begins from the perspective of the "other" and presents not only contemporary African American characters but historical figures and characters from other cultures. Parks adapted Nathaniel Hawthorne's *The Scarlet Letter* in two plays, *In the Blood* (1999) and *Fucking A* (2000). *In the Blood* features Hester as a woman who lives under an overpass with her five multiethnic, illegitimate children. The play stresses that identity and culture are becoming increasingly difficult to discover and claim, a condition that leads to disillusionment and diaspora. Hester is abandoned and ill treated by society and her lovers, and the play ends in tragedy. In *Fucking A*, Hester's "A" stands for abortionist. This play, too, ends in tragedy as Hester's son, who was a sweet youth, has become a violent and brutal man. In *Death of the Last Black Man*, Parks looks at language as a tool of oppression and expression. As Bernard mentions in her article on Parks's use of the musicality of language, the play reads like an example of slam poetry. There is no punctuation, and words are left out to run together to form their own unique rhythm (693). In Parks's play *Topdog/Underdog*, two brothers, Lincoln and Booth, struggle to achieve monetary independence. Lincoln once ran a three-card monte scam but has decided to earn his living by honest labor. He becomes an actor at the local arcade, impersonating Abraham Lincoln and re-enacting Lincoln's death. Booth decides to earn money by learning Lincoln's card tricks and setting up his own three-card monte business. The brothers argue frequently, culminating in Booth murdering Lincoln over a card game. As Bernard clearly states, Parks's figures are allegorical rather than realistic characters and reflect a double consciousness, or what Cornel West calls the postmodern condition (Bernard 690). Parks is less interested in having her plays construct meaning. Rather, she prefers that readers/viewers experience the images and language and draw their own conclusions (691). As Liz Diamond, who has directed several of her plays, said in an interview, "In Parks' world, the history is too vast, the characters too small for any psychological constructed character to have any impact" (Druckman 61).

Her play *Venus* premiered in 1995 at the Yale Repertory Theatre. In the play, Parks uses music to help her in her writing with Venus. She uses opera, often leaving out words and letting them run together to find their own rhymes (Solomon 76).

I will first begin by describing the format of the play script. Then I will show that specific African tropes—metaphors and techniques of performance—are contained in the script and performance, revealing a dual signifying system. I will then provide examples of language Parks uses to support my contention that the play functions in a stage of intercultural liminality.[1] Finally, I will pose questions about whose history this play addresses and to what extent this play evokes an African as much as an American worldview.

Venus, the play, appears to incorporate two performative devices—Brechtian alienation and African storytelling. These devices are merged in a format that Parks often uses in her plays, which is to create a production resembling a musical composition. The script contains moments of improvisation, vocal repetition, choral passages, and syncopated dialogue. Parks's plays are often organized in a series of scenes, sometimes hosted by a narrator who contributes historical context and dramatic commentary. At the same time, audiences are encouraged to participate in the process of telling the story. This merging of two performative devices—a Brechtian alienation effect of breaking into and out of the dramatic play structure with African storytelling techniques of telling and retelling a story using the participation of audience members—provides a double signifying mechanism. The audience (or readers) can, on the one hand, distance themselves from the action and ethos of the play by being re-minded that the characters are artificially constructed, yet, on the other hand, they can openly participate in the process of telling the story and empathizing with the main character's predicament.

The Brechtian alienation effect is clearly accentuated from the begin-ning of the play. Scenes are listed in reverse chronological order begin-ning with an "overture." During the intermission a scene continues to be played out as audience members either choose to remain in their seats or leave. A play within the play takes place, and performers address the audience directly. Parks allows directors to make optional cuts from her script for production purposes and offers them opportunities to fill in moments of stage time when no action or stage business is called for (she calls them "spells"). Finally, she puts historical footnotes in her written

Figure 3.1.   Adina Porter as Venus in the 1996 Richard Foreman production at the Yale Rep. Photo by Charlie Erickson.

script and provides a glossary of medical terms. With all these devices, Parks has alienated the audience member and reader by simultaneously garnering empathy for the principal character yet at the same time forcing the observer to evaluate the historical context. The effect is to provide a critical assessment of the Sara Baartman phenomenon and to engender a degree of empathy for her. Because the real-life issue of returning her remains to her homeland in South Africa was still being debated when the play opened in 1995, the connection between her stage life and real life was immediately apparent and supported Brecht's concept of why drama should be instructive and applicable to contemporary existence.

The play retells the story of a Khoikhoi woman who as a teenager is seduced into traveling to England and promised material wealth in return for becoming an exotic dancer. The dance performance, of course, turns out not to be of any artistic value to European audiences but rather produces a voyeuristic fascination for her freakish body (as in the real-life Sara Baartman). Venus is exhibited as an animal circus act with a special focus on parts of her anatomy such as her protruding buttocks. The characters announce themselves in the opening scene before presenting the star of the show—Venus. Only the star of the show is dead, and the narrator, called the Negro Resurrectionist, is forced to change the program, go back in time, and retell the tragic story of this woman who died suddenly at the age of twenty-five. Using the format of a journey play, Parks retells the story of Venus beginning with her childhood and ending up in Paris, France, where she is impregnated with her second child by a French lover, the Baron Docteur. She has been virtually kidnapped from South Africa and brought to England where she was given over to a sadistic woman, the Mother Showman. The Mother Showman dupes Venus into believing she will become rich as an exotic dancer and forces her to wear demeaning outfits, revealing her freakish body to fascinated British audiences in London.

A chorus of performers act as narrators of the story as they play different roles in her short life. They begin as the "Eight Human Wonders of the World," a bitterly sarcastic depiction of their roles as deformed human beings who exhibit themselves publicly. They later turn into witnesses in a court case involving a charge of indecency against Venus. The Baron Docteur, a kind of quack doctor in France, takes pity on Venus and buys her services from the Mother Showman. They subsequently fall in love; he has a child with her and in vain tries to protect her from the voyeuristic public who want to see more of her freak act. Finally, she succumbs to a disease that kills her at a young age. The closing scene has Venus inviting the audience to view her dead body as the Negro Resurrectionist reassures her that she still remains a star to the audience.

The play, divided into thirty-one scenes, suggests a musical piece with one scene stopping and the next one picking up in a different motif. In an interview, Parks remarked that she saw her plays as musically influenced and that opera had been her inspiration for this play. Venus is sometimes even referred to as a diva. The scenes are connected loosely by a narrator and chorus who provide commentary directly to the audience. There are other scenes, however, that are built from an image and are repeated at different stages in the play. The scenes of Venus's dead body being dissected are interspersed throughout the play, particularly for an extended period during the intermission. What perhaps also gives the form of this play an operatic quality are the rapid exchanges of dialogue in a kind of recitative style and moments of prolonged silence suggesting some musical interlude while the characters are relating. There is also a play-within-a-play ("For the Love of the Venus") that functions as a kind of parody of European exploitative desires in Africa and how they reflect a fascination for the exotic in African culture. A young bride-to-be tries to get her fiancé to notice her by walking differently to accentuate her large buttocks.

African storytelling techniques are applied throughout the play and provide opportunities for the audience to participate in the process. The opening scene calls for the audience to participate in the unfolding yarn of an unfortunate woman. Characters introduce themselves, and the chorus starts up a chant and announces the arrival of the star of the show, Venus. The chorus, which embodies different groups of characters, extols the audience to share in the experience and bond with the performers directly by reminding them that they know what is in store for this woman. The "chorus" is a familiar presence in what westerners called Kuntu Drama of the African Continuum. A chorus can be otherworldly and personify the dead or the living (Bernard 691). In effect, the story has been told before and is being retold so that future generations can experience the story and find lessons in it.

Some of the characters appear as types familiar in African stories. The character of the Mother Showman, an opportunistic woman who will if necessary exploit her own family for financial gain, is familiar because women in many parts of Africa are essential to maintaining an effective economy. The character of the Negro Resurrectionist is a kind of spiritualist who comments on the historical context and urges the audience to respond. The chorus transforms itself to a group of deformed freaks, then to spectators, then to members of a court, and finally to a medical team of anatomy specialists. The concept of a chorus representing different societal castes is another device used in African storytelling. Finally, there is a play-within-a-play ("For the Love of Venus") that comments on the action of the principal narrative. Throughout the play, the audience is consulted about the story, included in some of the songs and chants, and reminded of the historical context of the play. These devices suggest an Africanist framework for telling and retelling this story.

The metaphysical framework is important in understanding various scenes. For example, the opening scene reveals that Venus never got a proper burial. Within many African cultures, to be refused proper burial means you are cut off from your community of ancestors, essentially representing a kind of Christian hell. The whole concept of deformity suggests a tension between the spiritual and natural worlds. Among many African groups, notably the Yoruba of Nigeria, the worlds of the natural and the spiritual are strictly divided. Sickness, for example, can be cured with natural remedies based on spiritual needs, and physical deformity is often considered a problem related to a metaphysical spiritual deviation. "The Chorus of Eight Human Wonders" is a spiritual metaphor for a diseased world, a kind of spiritual plague. A Western view would suggest that deformity is a natural occurrence and should be regarded as a scientific phenomenon.

Another African trope occurs in the play-within-a-play. The characters of the Bride-to-Be and the Man, played by non-European actors, parody the nineteenth-century escapism of explorers who purportedly fall in love not only with African culture but "with something wild," presumably an African woman. African humor is often presented at the expense of the uncouth and naive European colonizer (see Soyinka's *Death and the King's Horseman*, Scene 2, 23–34) who shows no interest in another culture except as related to his or her perspective. The issue with Venus is that a character emerges who is not real but alienated in the Brechtian sense. She is a performative being—endowed with physical and psychological attributes but nevertheless regarded as a creature, and an ugly one, by many. There is a binary operating between the real Sara Baartman, the

Venus Hottentot, and the character represented by Parks in her play. The real Sarah Baartman is largely unknown as a psychological character. Baartman is obviously a victim and exploited, but the details of her individual relationships with her various oppressors are unsubstantiated. The Venus in Suzan-Lori Parks's play is a woman who stands on her own and speaks for herself. She is alienated, however, because the other characters are types who turn into nightmarish reincarnations from her tragic life.

I now want to comment on the language Parks uses. I mentioned a liminal state of intercultural interaction, which evokes Victor Turner's definition as a kind of breach between a natural occurrence and a social response. In terms of intercultural communication, the liminal state can refer to the space where cultures find common ground through mutually understood concepts. Sign language, religious rituals, and dress are areas where cultures evaluate each other and make decisions of how to proceed further. Parks, an African American woman, uses words that are emotionally evocative in American culture but also have resonance in African culture. Characters comment on the phenomenon of the Venus Hottentot by reciting a kind of musical phrase such as "diggidy-diggidy" and "hubba-hubba-hubba." These kinds of vocal riffs suggest an audience response to a show and connote men approvingly viewing a sexualized woman. African audiences who respond to these scenes do not necessarily read the same connotation into the performances, but the phrases nevertheless reinforce a tradition of vocally responding to live performance without using actual words.

The word "Venus" is common in both cultures, primarily as a Christian name, but combining it with the words "Black" and "goddess" suggests an exotic creature. Venus, the character, is also referred to as the "Dancing African Princess," which alludes to a designation for African exoticism that is different from African American. One is a "Princess," and the other is a goddess. When the chorus of eight human wonders appears as a group of deformed freaks, they walk in a chain gang, which evokes groups of slaves led to work each day. The concept of big buttocks may initially seem attractive in an American context, but if they are too large, they become a distortion. In Africa, big buttocks are not regarded purely as an aesthetically pleasing part of the body but have a practical application as well. Women in some African cultures carry items (even children) on their buttocks and use the muscles in that part of the body for transporting wares. The language in the historical excerpts and the scenes of dismembering her body has a cold, passionless quality. This is in contrast to the almost childlike exuberance of her speech and the rhythmic qualities of the chorus and narrator. There is even a scene where the Baron tried to teach French to Venus, and she reads like a child about the history and delicacy of chocolate.

It appears that Parks tries to use various layers of language to distinguish characters. In much the same way, African American writers have used language and musical motifs to evoke a culture. Baraka's *Slave Ship*, a one-act, showed how a few words could be used to represent a group of slaves being forcibly abducted and sent across the Atlantic. Her African characters are written in naive but literal language, whereas the European characters speak in a multilayered context. Words do not always mean what they are intended to mean. Venus, on the other hand, is open and honest, asking to be kissed, to be loved, and to be celebrated.

So whom does the play's history finally address? Is it about the early Victorian period when the scramble for Africa was on? Is it about the rape—literally and figuratively—of the African continent by European colonizers? Is it about an African female body and how it possesses unique anatomical qualities? Perhaps one needs to begin by exploring the various perspectives of gender identification. First, there is the perspective of women—especially women who perceive themselves as marginalized. This includes women (Latina, Asian American, African American) whose behavior has been traditionally stereotyped and whose bodies are objectified. I can point easily to a number of playwrights dealing with this question in plays including the above-mentioned *M. Butterfly* by David Henry Hwang and *Fur* by Migdalia Crux. Both playwrights have examined the ideal of Asian and Latina bodies written from a patriarchal perspective. Then, there is the perspective of an African American viewer (male or female) who sees the Venus Hottentot as a metaphor for discrimination against fully developed women. In their article, Stephens and Phillips divided African American women into stereotypical sexual scripts featuring "divas, aunt jeminas, golddiggers, and freaks," among others. The (mis)reading of an African American female body is central to their discussion.

Finally, there is the perspective of the Khoikhoi culture on what exactly this phenomenon of the Venus Hottentot really meant. Is the single case a representation of discrimination against all Khoikhoi peoples or is she just part of the larger charade of codifying African behavior? In interviews, Parks often bridled at the idea that she wrote only about African American issues and was labeled a Black feminist writer. She said that she was expected to write only about Black women and give them a voice through her plays. When she wrote *Top Dog/Under Dog*, however, her audience realized that her writing extended far beyond gender and race.

So what does this play address? Parks has insisted that the discovery (or "digging," as she likes to term it) is more important than some definitive meaning. My digging reveals that the demeaning experience of African women—and in particular, Khoikhoi women—at the hands of racist Europeans still reverberates today in the scholarly work of Black female sexuality. I have discovered that the liminal state between African and African American cultures lies not only between the languages but in the performative tropes for telling a story. I have discovered that playwrights like Suzan-Lori Parks work in an area of intercultural performance that can produce a Brechtian alienation effect on one hand and a statement of social testimony on the other. And, finally, in what Alissa Solomon calls "signifying the signifying," the play creates metaphoric language that reverberates in both African and African American cultures.

Venus lives on.

Ruined is a new play by Lynn Nottage, the author of *Intimate Apparel* and *Crumbs from the Table of Joy*. Nottage often writes about African American women but more recently has focused on topics associated with Africa. In *Ruined*, Nottage tackles the subject of the recent civil wars in the Congo from the point of view of a group of women led by the proudly contemptuous Mama Nadi, a war profiteer who runs a bar and bordello in a rural area of eastern Congo. She services men from all stripes—soldiers, European businessmen, and local miners. She runs her business with a stern hand but also manipulates her clientele and group of young female "employees" who are pressed into service by being promised food, shelter, and safety from marauding soldiers who rape and pillage at will. "Ruined" refers to a description of a woman who has been repeatedly raped and is no longer a prized commodity in the sex trade.

Nottage has structured her play with a conscious acknowledgment to Bertolt Brecht, whose *Mother Courage* offers many parallels to this play. In addition, the main character has similar character traits to Anna Fierling (Mother Courage), such as arrogance, cynicism, and a manipulative nature. Nottage also uses a character functioning as a kind of spiritual narrator to sing a litany of songs about war as the events unfold in the play. The male actors often play interchangeable roles (sometimes they play ordinary soldiers; other times they play villagers or commanders) representing the playwright's desire to evoke a fractured patriarchal society. The play, however, doesn't strive to create the Brechtian alienation effect because the narrative follows a linear plotline and the characters do not step out of the play to address the audience.

The vast land area known as the Congo has been mythologized by Europeans ever since the corrupt and cruel Leopold II of Belgium raped the country of its resources. The land was often dismissed as representative of "darkest Africa." Yet, this area became the richest source of raw materials on the continent, and the Europeans exploited the land and its peoples to the fullest extent during and after "the scramble for Africa." During the twentieth century, Congolese leaders who resisted colonial rule or acquiesced to their power often became symbols of revolutionary zeal (as in the case of Patrice Lumumba) or were demonized as corrupt dictators (as in the case of Mobutu Sese Seko). The recent civil wars that culminated in a democratically elected government in 2006 have not stopped the fighting between government troops and a renegade general named Laurent Nkunda. The battles of warring militias are not fought over government policy but over proceeds of rural mines producing tin ore and other minerals.

Ever since the Rwandan genocide in 1994, the neighbors of the Congo have played a major role in destabilizing the country. Thousands of Hutu refugees swarmed into neighboring Congo. In the province of Orientale (where *Ruined* is set), an alliance of Congolese groups opposed to Mobutu was formed in 1996 with the help of Uganda. Calling themselves the Alliance of Congolese Groups opposed to Mobutu (ADL), they used weapons not only to kill opposing government forces but to protect the industry of coltran, a mineral compound used in the production of mobile phones and high-tech consumer goods. Later in 1998, a group calling themselves the RCD-Goma, with support from the primarily Tutsi government in Rwanda, launched another war against Congolese government forces, this time headed by Laurent Kabila. It is suggested that the majority of rapes committed against women of mainly Hunde and Nande ethnicities were by members of militias from the RCD-Goma group.

Nottage wanted to tell the story of these ravaged Congolese women and conducted numerous interviews with actual survivors. According to John Holmes, the United Nations undersecretary general, the sexual violence of the Congo is the worst and most brutal in the world. The play follows the lives of individuals who use Mama Nadi's bar as a kind of temporary refuge from the violence and killing outside but find that associating with this haughty, self-absorbed businesswoman has its price. Her daughter, Josephine, is one of the prostitutes hoping to move into the big city and marry a European. Salima, a mother and wife of an army draftee, Fortune, is brought in by a street salesman, Christian, along with his niece, Sophie. Salima has already received her share of sexual torture, including being tied to a tree and repeatedly raped. Sophie, the young observer of the action (and, perhaps, Nottage's alter ego) has already been "ruined" and has a pronounced limp. She, however, can sing beautifully (which she does throughout the play) and can read and write and help with the business. Salima, however, is the plainer of the two, and Sophie with her inquiring doe eyes and innocent demeanor becomes the favorite of many of the male customers even though Salima and Josephine must perform the majority of the work. The men who hang around the bar, and who count Mama Nadi as a friend, include Christian, who is a participant and victim of a corrupt system of bartering and stealing, and Mr. Harari, who is a Mediterranean jeweler and black marketeer. Both men find refuge in the bar, although Christian, for a reason that is not always clear, has developed a liking for the irascible owner of the bar and tries to convince her to start a legitimate business.

Nottage seems to suggest that the pristine Congolese world of spiritual interaction and family ties survives even when confronted with commercial and destructive forces from the outside. Josephine still proudly reveals that her father is a chief, and the other women still talk longingly of nature, family, and a peaceful coexistence. Mama Nadi, however, dashes the young women's hopes with her cynical comments: "Yeah, and my father was whoever put money in my moma's pocket. Chief, farmer, who the hell cares?" (n.p.). Later on, she evokes her own mother's opportunist nature, which she has inherited: "My mother taught me that you can follow behind everyone and walk in the dust, or you can walk ahead through the unbroken thorny bush. You may get blood on your ankles, but you arrive first and not covered in the residue of others" (n.p.).

The staging of *Ruined* seems to consciously draw from African story-telling techniques. For example, despite the naturalistic setting, characters sing and dance as well as tell stories. Sophie's lyrics often have the feel of cynical cabaret songs from the 1920s but are sung with freshness and exuberance like a griot foretelling the future:

> You come here to forget,
> You say drive away all regret
> And dance like it's the ending
> The ending of the war.
>
> But, can the music be all forgiving
> Purge the wear and tear of the living?
> Will the sound drown out your sorrow,
> So you'll remember nothing tomorrow?

This storytelling technique allows the singer to comment on the action but also brings the audience into the performance. Dances and songs are familiar to the audience and allow them to participate as they would in a religious festival where an ongoing conversation takes place between spiritual leaders and their congregations. This technique has its own alienation effect in the sense that the universality of surviving war turns this play into a referendum on gender violence in times of war. Indeed, the bodies of women once again become the source for violence and destructive behavior, especially as seen through the eyes of a woman who has overcome her "ruined" status by selling her soul instead. In "Wasn't Brecht an African Writer?" Sandra L. Richards suggests that Brecht's alienation effect (when actors often comment about their characters either directly or vicariously) has been often used in African performance and may very well predate his application of it by hundreds of years.

By the end of Act I, the characters in *Ruined* have grown more desperate as the situation worsens. Characters can no longer verbalize their frustrations and resort to other forms of physical and psychological release. Christian, who has sworn off liquor for many years, returns to drinking and finds a drunken stupor to be the easiest place to hide his pain. Fortune tries desperately to find his wife, and when he hears she might be working at Mama Nadi's, he implores Mama Nadi to produce his wife, which she refuses to do. Josephine begins to dance wildly to exorcise her own frustrated dreams of sophisticated city life, and Sophie, who has embezzled some money from her controlling boss to help pay for an operation to repair the damage to her sexual organs, is exposed by her employer and is almost thrown out of the bar for good. Yet, there is still hope. Mama Nadi decides to keep her prized possession and marvels at Sophie's audacity and cleverness, joining her favorite employee in a rousing song celebrating the eternal warrior in Congolese mythology:

> Hey Monsieur,
> Come play, Monsieur,
> Hey Monsieur,
> Come play, Monsieur,
>
> The Congo sky rages electric,
> As bullets fly like hell's rain,
> Wild flowers wilt, and the forest decays,
> But here we're pouring Champagne.
>
> 'Cuz a warrior knows no peace,
> When a hungry lion's awake,
> But when that lion's asleep,
> The warrior is free to play.
>
> Drape your weariness on my shoulder,
> Sweep travel dust from your heart,
> Villages die as soldiers grow bolder,
> We party as the world falls apart.

As the second act unfolds, one realizes that Mama Nadi's "refuge" is crumbling and the violence and destruction of the civil war outside has come in to extract its victims. Both the rebel leader, Jerome Kisembe, and the government forces leader, Commander Osembenga, converge again at the bar, although at different times. Salima, in a final gesture of defiance, has fought back against her captors and is dying from wounds as her husband, Fortune, is belatedly reunited with her. Mama Nadi, in a gesture of immense generosity, takes a precious stone she has saved and asks Mr. Harari to take Sophie away and sell the stone to pay for the operation she needs. Again, by the time Sophie is free to go, Harari and his frightened driver have left and Sophie is left behind.

Nottage, perhaps, cannot end her engrossing play with a bitter and cynical aftertaste that mirrors the real-life ending of the Congolese civil war. There is a ceasefire, but the new "democracy" is a fragile arrangement and probably only temporary. Instead, Nottage gives the play a moralistic tone by having Mama Nadi and Christian reconcile and decide to carve out a living together in this desolate environment. The moral is that love and companionship, along with strong spiritual values, can overcome all kinds of evil. War may be hell, but there is a purgatory waiting for people at the camp of the UN Peacekeeping Force. Then, later there may be a heaven waiting. As Jean-Paul Sartre so famously wrote in his play *No Exit*, "Hell is other people." One anticipates that Mama Nadi, Christian, and the group of survivors from the bar may indeed end up in that existential hotel room for all eternity. Instead, Nottage has remained optimistic and hopeful and has freed her hostages.

If Venus still lives in our hearts, so does Mama Nadi. Both women trafficked in Black women's bodies—one, victimized and naive, sells herself, and the other, cynical and manipulative, sells women's bodies as a commercial tool for economic survival. Ironically, the less spiritual woman who has little room for God and family ends up making a change in her life and finds a measure of peace. In the world of mythologizing Africa, identifying a measure of peace and prosperity is an enticing perspective. The world might want more leaders like the charismatic Nelson Mandela, but finding them and writing about them might prove to be far more elusive.

NOTE

1. I refer to Victor Turner's use of the "liminal state" in "Betwixt and Between."

WORKS CITED

Baraka, Amiri. *Slave Ship: A Historical Pageant*. Newark, NJ: Jihad Publishing House, 1969.

Bernard, Louise. "The Musicality of Language: Redefining History in Suzan-Lori Parks's *The Death of the Last Black Man in the Whole Entire World*." *African American Review* 31.4 (1997): 687–98. Print.

Chambers, Robert. *The Book of Days: A Miscellany of Popular Antiquities in Connection with the Calendar, Including Anecdote, Biography, History, Curiosities of Literature and Oddities of Human Life and Character*. London: W&R Chambers, 1832. Print.

Druckman, Steven. "Suzan-Lori Parks and Liz Diamond: Doo-a-didly-dit-dit." *Drama Review* 39.3 (Fall 1996): 56–75. Print.

Gilman, Sander. "Black Bodies, White Bodies: Toward an Iconography of Female Sexuality in Late Nineteenth-Century Art, Medicine, and Literature." *Critical Inquiry* 12 (Autumn 1985): 204–42. Print.

Hammonds, Evelynn M. "Toward a Genealogy of Black Female Sexuality: The Problematic of Silence." *Feminist Genealogies, Colonial Legacies, and Democratic Futures*. Ed. M. Jacqui Alexander and Chandra Talpade Mohanty. New York: Routledge, 1997. 170–82. Print.

Parks, Suzan-Lori. *The American Play and Other Works*. New York: Theatre Communications Group, 1995. Print.

———. *TopDog/Underdog*. New York: Theatre Communications Group, 1999. Print.

———. *Venus*. New York: Theatre Communications Group, 1997. Print.

Rayner, Alice, and Harry J. Elam Jr. "Unfinished Business: Reconfiguring History in Suzan-Lori Parks's *The Death of the Last Black Man in the Whole Entire World*." *Theatre Journal* 46 (1994): 447–61. Print.

Richards, Sandra. "Wasn't Brecht an American Writer?" *Brecht in Asia and Africa: The Brecht Yearbook XIV*. Hong Kong: U of Hong Kong, 1989. 168–83.

Solomon, Alisa. "Signifying on the Signifin': The Plays of Suzan-Lori Parks." *Theater* 21.3 (1990): 73–80. Print.

Soyinka, Wole. *Death and the King's Horseman*. New York: W. W. Norton, 1975.

Spillers, Hortense. "Interstices: A Small Drama of Words." *Pleasure and Danger: Exploring Female Sexuality*. Ed. Carole S. Vance. London: Pandora, 1984. 73–100. Print.

Stephens, Dionne P., and Layli D. Phillips. "Freaks, Gold Diggers, Divas, and Dykes: The Sociohistorical Development of Adolescent African American Women's Sexual Scripts." *Sexuality and Culture* 7.1 (January 2003): 3–49. Print.

Strother, Zoë. "Display of the Body Hottentot." *Africans on Stage*. Ed. Bernth Lindfors. Bloomington: Indiana UP, 1999. 1–61. Print.

Turner, Victor. "Betwixt and Between: The Liminal Period in Rites de Passage." *The Forest of Symbols*. Ithaca, NY: Cornell UP, 1967.

4

THE CODIFICATION OF SOUL IN AFRICAN-DERIVED DANCE CULTURE

Benita Brown

All Things JuJu[1]

Have you ever arrived at a fork in the road (literally or figuratively) and became confused about which path to take?
Have you been privy to the illusion of the rainbow?
Were you in awe of its majesty?
Have you heard the whisper of Africa through the voice of the Egyptian Goddess Auset?
Have you witnessed the power of Qya as she summons her strength and manifests herself as a tornado or hurricane?
Were you smitten with fear?
Did you pay deference to her strength by removing yourself from her path?
Have you witnessed the energy of electricity in its original form?
A Thunderbolt!
It soars through space
Releasing and giving energy
Communicating with humanity through light and sound
Shango! He embodies vocal chords when striking!?
Do you remember hearing the elders say: That's God talking!
Oba Koso, Shango! The King Is not Dead
At the polar opposite . . .
Have you experienced the serenity of the ocean?
Have you been enchanted by the movement of the river?
Have you been in love?

Have you enjoyed good health?
Have you been blessed with good fortune?
After all is said and done . . .
Have you danced your dance?
(Un)consciously rekindling your African past
Do you know if you have danced the dance of the ancestors?
Does dance kindle euphoria for you as observer or participant?
Considering James Brown's creed: I got soul and I'm Super Bad!
Do you have soul? Are you Super Bad?
Yes!?
Then you have experienced the manifestations of the Òrìsà
Their various characteristics and attributes are the reincarnate of humanity
The Òrìsà are dramatized through African-derived theatrical, mythological, and folkloric performances staged by human beings: the holistic world stage is set for conquering and equalizing life's complexities while cosmic dances are (re)created as the vehicle for direct communications with the Gods!
—Benita Brown

In African American communities, African-derived dance, music, song, clothing, oratory, and foodstuffs reflect the sociocultural, economic, political, religious, and spiritual environment of the immediate, surrounding, and extended community. Cultural practices factor in a cadre of African-derived mythology and folklore that oftentimes calls upon dance and music to invoke the spirit and appease the soul as a way of coping with hardships bringing joy, peace, and happiness into the community. Looking into African-derived mythology and folklore, one may find that these cultural elements carry messages that come from the ancestors and/ or deities and may include advice and problem-solving scenarios in answer to issues affecting the community. Many times in response to economic, political, and even religious maladies, performing artists create dance, music, song, and drama as a way to inform and educate as well as eradicate that which may be deemed as evil by uplifting the spirit and feeding positivity into the soul of the community. African American audiences, performers, and performances become part of a supernatural force that is spiritual in nature and depends heavily on the belief systems and practices of the ancestors. This soulful triad is evident in the creative and historical dances of African American performers. Consider Katherine Dunham's *Shango* (1945), Geoffrey Holder's *Douglas* (1974), Arthur

Hall's *Ode to Yemaya* (1975), Kulu Mele's *Oshun* (2010), and Bill T. Jones's Tony Award–winning Broadway musical hit *Fela* (2010). Each one of these artists, born and raised in America, reached back into their African ancestry to create African-derived, kinesthetic dance movements that enlivened the deities and continued the connection between the ancestors and those that are in the land of the living. Each of these artists created renditions of dances in honor of African ancestors and deities regardless of his or her personal set of religious beliefs.

African American artists have relied heavily on mythology and folklore incorporating spirit and soul to communicate to their audiences. Fitting into the aesthetic theory and practice of Africa, audience members become a part of the performance and are so inclined to offer their own artistic contributions as oratory, signifying, participatory behavior that spiritually/soulfully enhances the performance. Invoking the spirit and going deep inside the soul of the performer, especially in dance, is where the performer re-enacts mythological figures showing off the power and prowess of their African ancestors. Hence, many African Americans defer to the spirit and soul of the dance, as dance is the amulet of sacred and secular practices among African Americans. African-derived dance brings about the spirit and soul, and it is the juju African Americans use to symbolize, codify, signify, and invoke their ancestral roots.

SPIRIT AND SOUL IN AFRICAN-DERIVED DANCE

What is spirit and what is soul? Although these may be nebulous terms for many, African Americans have a strong proclivity toward the spirit and soul, partly due to their strong cultural beliefs in ancestral deference. The (un)conscious cultural practice of building shrines to loved ones who have passed away is just one of the many ways that African-derived ancestral deference continues. The purpose of the shrine is to appease the spirit and soul of the person who passed away. In Bill T. Jones's *Fela*, his late mother was depicted as an omnipresent medium to guide him through his most tumultuous times. Performing artists from the grassroots level to Broadway speak about a spiritual realm or soulful feeling in connection with creativity, especially in dance. To speak about soul and spirit can be difficult because of they are, for the most part, intangible, but they are tangible in African-derived dance and music. In Yoruba cosmology and pantheon, for example, the (un)conscious devotees of the *Òrìsà* found among African Americans involve themselves in ecstatic dance. In her article "Embodied Knowledge in African American Dance Performance," Yvonne Daniel states:

> Devotees within this and similar African American religious practices in Haiti, Brazil, and the United States understand the function of dance performance as a primary vehicle for spiritual communication, physical [and mental] healing, and social balance. Through their bodies, they access and store music and dance scores. These scores, however, relate to belief, politics, and economics, and not simply to social relaxation. . . . Devotees interpret the stories of dancing divinities called Orichas (or *Òrìsà*) as statements on human behavior. (n.p.)

Thus, the author proposes the following tenets in relationship to spirit and soul: (1) soul inspirits a nonphysical and unseen entity, (2) soul is the core of the heart and the source of the heartbeat, (3) the spirit is an offshoot of the soul, (4) the soul and spirit are surrealistic, (5) soul and spirit are euphoric, and (6) soul and spirit are the main ingredients of style in African American dance culture. Put succinctly, soul is metaphorical and spirit is metaphysical. Spirit thrives on emotive responses from human beings; thus, it reveals itself as a result of physical stimuli from within the surrounding environment. This is how soul and spirit animate the dance movements that are performed in conjunction with particular scores of music and words of a song. This cultural phenomenon originates at the grassroots level; in fact, it is the attributive and birthplace of popular culture among African Americans. In humanistic terms, soul and spirit communicate elements of style in African American dance culture.

There are dimensionalities of the spirit(s), such as those of the survivalist spirit as it manifests itself through dance, music, and song, thus keeping alive undercurrents of mythology and folklore in grassroots dance culture. Donna Marimba Richards states, "African ritual drama, (including dance) wherever it is found, is an affirmation of humanness" (29).

In *Let the Circle Be Unbroken*, Donna Marimba Richards states:

> The idea of "spirit" is especially important for an appreciation of the African American experience. "Spirit" is, of course, not a rationalistic concept. It cannot be quantified, measured, explained by or reduced to

neat rational, conceptual categories as European thought demands. Spirit is ethereal. It is neither "touched" nor "moved," "seen" nor "felt" in the way that physical entities are touched, moved, seen and felt. (3)

THE RING SHOUT: AN AMULET FOR AFRICAN-DERIVED SACRED AND SECULAR DANCE

In his book, *African Cultural Values: An Introduction* (1996), Kwame Gyekye states: "One outstanding feature of artistic performances such as music and dance is their participatory character: music-making and dancing are communal activities, aimed—apart from their purely aesthetic qualities—at deepening communal sentiments and consciousness" (178).

The importance of the reciprocal relationship between music and dance lies in the lyrics of the song accompanied by the rhythmic structure and musical instrumentation. Music in African and African American culture reflects political, sociocultural, and economic importance. The song and its words direct the movements of the dance. The song is as important, if not more important, than the accompanying instrumentation. The relationship between song and dance is highlighted in the call-and-response idiom prevalent in African and African American culture in dance and music.

The African American cultural continuum of the dance called the ring shout used soul and spirit as a survivalist technique seen in various dance forms at the grassroots level among African Americans. Paul Carter Harrison, in *Kuntu Drama* (1974), states: "Theater is a spiritualized secular event that finds its juxtaposition within the sacred institutional framework of the African American church" (37). Harrison is speaking about theatre; however, dance and music are applicable because they are included within theatre.

The spiritual sustenance and creation of emotive responses are often linked to exposure to music, song, and dance. Dance movements using the head, torso, limbs, and pelvis, coupled with expressive hand and face gestures, reveal the results of internal stimuli created by music and song. Thus, it seems that the components of dance are first internalized. These feelings are then externalized, creating visual stimulants shared by the community. The dance and the dancer lift up the innermost feelings of the immediate and surrounding community.

In *African Cultural Values: An Introduction*, Kwame Gyekye writes:

> Art in traditional African cultures has both functional and purely aesthetic dimensions. One outstanding feature of artistic performances such as music and dance is their participatory character: music-making and dancing are communal activities, aimed—apart from their purely aesthetic qualities—at deepening communal sentiments and consciousness. Among the criteria of aesthetic value and judgment are appropriateness and fittingness. Music, dancing, and even clothing must be appropriate to the occasion. Beauty is seen not only in works of art and in the human figure but also in human conduct, in humanity itself, and in a person's character. (178)

Leonard Barrett, author of *Soul-Force*, describes it as follows: "Soul-force is that power of the Black man that turns sorrow into joy, crying into laughter, defeat into victory. It is patience while suffering, determination while frustrated and hope while in despair. It derives its impetus from the ancestral heritage of Africa, its refinement from the bondage of slavery, and its continuing vitality from the conflict of the present" (2).

Further, in *Let the Circle Be Unbroken*, Donna Marimba Richards states: "'Soul-Force' is the basic ingredient of Black survival" (34). Consider the European-American Christian doctrine: "One must be free of sin in order to save one's soul." In the African American grassroots experience, soul has an overarching, metaphorical function. It is more than the notion of Negritude, just as it is more than strictly religious. Undeniably, the role of the Black Church heightens one's awareness of the Almighty God; however, as Richards, Barrett, and others have expressed, soul is a sociocultural and political survival mechanism. It inspires African American belief systems and values in the face of opposition and degradation. According to Barrett: "Soul signifies the moral and emotional fiber of the Black man," giving him "strength, power, intense effort and will to live" (1).

THE SHOUT

I contend that the dances called the "bop" and perhaps the "slop" are the kinesthetic movements left over from our African ancestry (including the dance movements from the worship of the *Òrìṣà*). The "shout" is a non-verbal but nonetheless highly communicative dance that appears on a highly spiritual realm.

The following is a description by Lincoln and Mamiya (1990) of how a "shout" occurred at an African American Christian gathering:

> After the regular religious services were over, or on special "praise nights," the benches in the early black churches or "praise houses" would be pushed back against the wall so that the dancing could begin. The dancers or "shouters," as they were called, would form a circle, and to the cadence of a favorite shout song or "running spiritual" would begin a slow, syncopated shuffling, jerking movement "bumped" by the handclapping or body slapping of those waiting on the sidelines. The tempo gradually quickened, and during the course of the dance (which might last for seven or eight hours), shouters who became possessed, or who dropped from sheer exhaustion, were immediately replaced by others waiting to take their places. (352)

At the turn of the century, among European Americans, the "shout" (also called "ring shout") was the most misunderstood cultural occurrence in dance. It was viewed as "barbaric" and "lascivious" because it was filled with "ritual dancing" and "spirit possession" (Lincoln and Mamiya 1990). Because European Americans considered this dance form "savage idol worship," African Americans sought to hide and disguise this spiritually filled dance in secret and sacred places (Lincoln and Mamiya 1990). As it traveled north in the African American community, the "shout" was disguised and sometimes took on different names. Speaking of how the "ring shout" was performed in Place Congo in New Orleans, Southern purports that these types of dances were a part of "the Pinkster dances in New York and the jubilees in Philadelphia" (138).

At the turn of the century, however, elite African Americans in Philadelphia despised these kinds of cultural practices because they reminded them of their African past, which they preferred to forget. The disdain that Bishop Daniel Alexander Payne of the African Methodist Episcopal Church in Philadelphia and founder of Wilberforce University had for the "ring shout" has been well documented. He called the dance "ridiculous and heathenish" (Lincoln and Mamiya 354). Even James Weldon Johnson, another famous Philadelphian, said that instances of the "shout" are "neither true spirituals nor truly religious"; they are "semi-barbaric remnants of primitive African dances" that are at best "quasi-religious" (Lincoln and Mamiya 354). The "shout," seemingly, was relegated to oblivion because of the pressures from inside and outside of the African American community. Yet, according to C. Eric Lincoln and Lawrence H. Mamiya, authors of *The Black Church in the African American Experience*, it was still alive in North Philadelphia in the 1960s. "Consigned to the 'abyss' with the spiritual, the 'ring dance' or the 'shout' has been largely abandoned, except in black Holiness and Pentecostal sects where forms of the 'holy dance' are still continued" (354). However, in the endnotes to chapter 12, "Music and the Church," Lincoln and Mamiya describe a form of the "shout" at a church located in North Philadelphia at Twelfth and Popular Streets during the late 1960s.

> One example of a modified "ring-shout" is found in the offertory ritual of Daddy Grace's United House of Prayer for All Peoples. With Bishop Daddy Grace William McCullough sitting on his elevated throne, the congregation formed a large circle and to the accompaniment of a brass band, members shuffled forward swaying from side to side and dropped their offering in collection plates at the front. As a form of offertory musical chairs, people who ran out of money sat down, while others continued. (464–65)

The "shout" or "ring shout" is a classic within the framework of African American dance culture manifested through various grassroots dance forms. The "shout" movement is evident not only in the "ring shout" but also in the improvisational movements historically found in the "cakewalk," "lindy hop," and "bop." The antecedents to these dances took on different names and paralleled each other in various parts of the country. Each dance has its basic movement structure, then there are inserted improvisational dance movements similar to shouting, and then the dancer returns to the basic movement structure staying in time with the rhythmic structure.

In African-based culture and philosophy God is present in everything, everywhere, at all times. According to Mbiti:

> Because traditional religions permeate all the departments of life, there is no formal distinction between the sacred and the secular, between the religious and non-religious, between the spiritual and the material areas of life. Wherever the African is, there is his religion: he carries it to the fields where he is sowing seeds or harvesting a new crop; he takes it with him to the beer party or to attend a funeral ceremony; and if he is educated, he takes religion with him to the examination room at school or in the university; if he is a politician he takes it to the house of parliament. (2)

This worldview was transported to the new world, carried by Africans to the shores of America. Thus, religious—or soulful—activity is not confined to Sunday morning worship but is prevalent throughout life. A beer garden or a North Philadelphia speakeasy, for example, may be the setting.

The presence of soul in African American culture is pervasive; however, it is frequently misinterpreted as irrational behavior. Westernized descriptions of African American cultural practices are wrought with demeaning misconceptions and stereotypical terminology. Terms such as heathenistic, immoral, primitive, uncivilized, and promiscuous have been used as descriptors. Richards posits the following:

> Emotional response, identification, and involvement became of less and less value, (in the Eurocentric worldview) until these tendencies, generated by a scientific word-view, affected peoples' abilities to feel and to express feeling. It is precisely that quality of human response to which the concept "soul" refers. . . . [T]hought and feeling are understood to be inextricable and to be necessary for an accurate perception of reality. (35)

It is important to understand that in most cases, African American creativity is intrinsically based on emotions that seek the approval and presence of the Holy Spirit in its myriad manifestations. Philosophical scholars have asserted the multifaceted presence of the Holy Spirit in African-based cultures. According to Mbiti's ontology, the Most High embodies nature, the cosmos, animate and inanimate objects, the universe, the ancestors, celestial beings, and human beings. Carlton Molette, author of "Afro-American Ritual Drama," states: "The Afro-American aesthetic places a very high value upon emotionally motivated behavior;

or another term that might be used to describe it . . . would be spiritually motivated behavior" (9).

In African American aesthetic modalities, dance is used as a communicative phenomenon that creates a spiritual connection that fosters the well-being of society. The connection between soul and spirit is an important facilitator of dance. The dancer executes movements that promote emotive responses from the participants and observers. Soul helps observers and participants confirm the community's connectedness because the dancer is a vehicle to the spiritual world. It is a belief system that connects to the dancer while she or he unites the community with the Most High.

Although the various elements of soul and spirit, in this context, are basically an African-based cultural phenomenon, the concept of soul surely exists in every culture. African American culture, however, takes on a definition that gives an emphatic depth and magnitude to the concept of soul, making it relative to social, economic, political, and cultural milieus and survivalist mechanisms.

In *Black Talk: Words and Phrases from the Hood to the Amen Corner*, Geneva Smitherman provides a definition of soul: "Soul: The essence of life, feeling, passion, emotional depth—all of which are believed to be derived from struggle, suffering, and having participated in the Black Experience. Having risen above the suffering, the person gains soul" (211). In *Working the Spirit: Ceremonies of the African Diaspora*, Joseph M. Murphy states: "The spirit moves individuals in particular ways, but never alone. The individual cannot manifest the spirit without the assistance of the community" (173–74).

The African American community reaffirms the presence of soul using dance as a channel to express closeness to the Holy Spirit. They confer these feelings by encouraging a movement style that is ultimately and openly judged by the community. Author Sule Greg Wilson in *The Drummer's Path: Moving the Spirit with Ritual and Traditional Drumming* gives us the following: "To achieve the ability to 'rock and roll' with the music, whether the full orchestra is there playing or not, you must 'digest' the rhythm into your own soul, into your spirit. Your nephesh, ka, electromagnetic body, your blood and aura, all have to strum (or 'note, strummey') with the beat" (43).

Suffice it to say that African Americans can claim a classic dance. That dance is the shout in its many forms and manifestations. Regardless of the African American's zealous ambition to learn and conquer continental African dances and even Europeanized ballroom dances that have been mixed with African American jazz dance, we have been successful in creating our own. Wilson sees the importance of identifying an African American cultural dance lineage as he states:

> Are you grounded enough in your own sacred music and folklore to reach a common ground? Can you play gospel tambourine, sing a blues lick? Do you know the classic tap steps, did you ever lindy hop, or bop, or do some kinda hand dance with your mamma and poppa? . . . Knowing where you come from keeps you safe and centered, like a trail of bread crumbs or twine, when you're delving in the realm of another. (15)

Further, Wilson contends: "All God's creations have power. To use power in Hetep (peace and harmony) you must accept yourself—you past, you culture and its contributions. Then you can bring them to the world, to help you learn the world. If you don't, you will always be searching, trying to fill up that hole in your sole [soul], made when you ignored who you are" (16).

The soul, the spirit, and the dance movements within the shout and ring shout continue to be of the utmost importance in defining African American aesthetics and culture. Soul music played a major role in the enlightenment of the community because it was based on a sacred premise in a secular world where time and space, mythology and folklore intertwined.

Kebede provides the following: "It is clear why music is closely related to religion in almost all African cultures. Music helps us to pass into other realms of consciousness. The heightened feeling enhanced by musical experience is aligned with spirituality and the other world—'the world in which things are no longer subject to time and space'" (quoted in Wilson 94).

Further, Olly Wilson states that the music experience is "a multimedia one in which many kinds of collective human output are inextricably linked. Hence, a typical traditional [African] ceremony will include music, dance, the plastic arts (in the form of elaborate masks and/or costumes) and perhaps ritualistic drama" (quoted in Maultsby 189).

African Americans continue to value and embrace an entire cultural lineage, both in the new world as well as the old through their

Figure 4.1.   Ama Schley, principal dancer of the Kulu Mele African Dance and Drum Ensemble of Philadelphia, performs the dance called Sofa, a war dance traditionally performed in Guinea, West Africa. Photo by Gabriel Bienczycki.

(un)conscious involvement with spirit and soul through dance and the (un)conscious connection to the ancestors and deities. The crossing of the Atlantic did not end African cultural belief systems and practices, especially in dance, but began a new culture combined with other cultural influences.

NOTE

1. My referencing JuJu is my way of linking the past and present whereby I pay homage to the ancestors and the deities through my scholarship in dance—specifically, African-derived, kinesthetic dance moves and culture based on West African mythology and folklore. Although it is common knowledge that some African Americans may find their ancestry in central and southern Africa, as mentioned in my article on the Òrìṣà Paradigm, "JuJu" is yet another term that connotes the mystical, magical, and supernatural occurrences as seen within the African Diaspora. This spiritual outlook and cultural practices have been very important as survival mechanisms for African Americans both historically and presently as they were imported from West Africa, although North, South, and

Figure 4.2.   The Kulu Mele African Dance and Drum Ensemble of Philadelphia performing a drum orchestration with the women of the group performing dance movements simultaneously. They are using the West African rhythm called Dun-Dun-Ba as it is played on the Djun-Djun (drums). The piece was choreographed (circa 2005) by Arisa Ingram. Also, pictured at the forefront is Dorothy Wilkie who is the artistic director of the company. Photo by Gabriel Bienczycki.

East Africa were not and are not devoid of such cultural practices and belief systems. Here I push the academic envelope of the study of Africa-derived mythology and folklore, contending—based on my observations and participation on social and sacred dancing as a professional and within grassroots cultural practices—that it has as its crux the presence of spirit and soul in social and sacred dancing among African Americans. It is my intent to open a flurry of academic discourse both pro and con concerning the theoretical basis of which I write.

WORKS CITED

Aschenbrenner, Joyce. *Katherine Dunham: Dancing a Life*. Urbana: U of Illinois P, 2002.
    Print.
Barrett, Leonard E. *Soul-Force: African Heritage in Afro-American Religion*. Garden City,
    NY: Anchor, 1974. Print.

Brown, David H. *Santería Enthroned: Art, Ritual, and Innovation in an Afro-Cuban Religion.* Chicago: U of Chicago P, 2003. Print.

Clarke, Peter B. *New Trends and Developments in African Religions.* Westport, CT: Greenwood, 1998. Print.

Costen, Melva Wilson. *In Spirit and in Truth: The Music of African American Worship.* Louisville, KY: Westminster John Knox, 2004. Print.

Daniel, Yvonne. "Embodied Knowledge in African American Dance Performance." *African Roots/American Culture: Africa in the Creation of the Americas.* Lanham: Rowman & Littlefield, 2001. Print.

DeFrantz, Thomas. *Dancing Revelations: Alvin Ailey's Embodiment of African American Culture.* Oxford: Oxford UP, 2004. Print.

Elam, Harry Justin, and David Krasner. *African-American Performance and Theater History: A Critical Reader.* Oxford: Oxford UP, 2001. Print.

Fabre, Geneviève, and Robert G. O'Meally. *History and Memory in African-American Culture.* New York: Oxford UP, 1994. Print.

Fernández Olmos, Margarite, and Lizabeth Paravisini-Gebert.. *Creole Religions of the Caribbean: An Introduction from Vodou and Santería to Obeah and Espiritismo.* New York: New York UP, 2003. Print.

———, eds. *Healing Cultures: Art and Religion as Curative Practices in the Caribbean and Its Diaspora.* New York: Palgrave, 2001. Print.

Glazier, Stephen D. *Encyclopedia of African and African-American Religions.* New York: Taylor and Francis, 2001. Print.

Gyekye, Kwame. *African Cultural Values: An Introduction.* Philadelphia: Sankofa, 1996. Print.

Harrison, Paul Carter. *Kuntu Drama: Plays of the African Continuum.* New York: Grove, 1974. Print.

Holmes, Barbara Ann. *Joy Unspeakable: Contemplative Practices of the Black Church.* Minneapolis: Fortress, 2004. Print.

Kempton, Arthur. *Boogaloo: The Quintessence of American Popular Music.* New York: Pantheon, 2003. Print.

Lincoln, C. Eric, and Lawrence H. Mamiya. *The Black Church in the African-American Experience.* Durham: Duke UP, 1990. Print.

Marini, Stephen A. *Sacred Song in America: Religion, Music, and Public Culture.* Urbana: U of Illinois P, 2003. Print.

Maultsby, Portia K. "Africanisms in African-American Music." *Africanisms in American Culture.* Ed. Joseph E. Holloway. Bloomington: Indiana UP, 1990. Print.

Mbiti, John S. *Introduction to African Religion.* 2nd ed. Portsmouth, NH: Heinemann Educational Publishers, 1991.

Molette, Carlton. "Afro-American Ritual Drama." N.p.: n.p., 1973. Print.

Murphy, Joseph M. *Working the Spirit: Ceremonies of the African Diaspora.* Boston: Beacon, 1994. Print.

Reed, Teresa L. *The Holy Profane: Religion in Black Popular Music.* Lexington: University of Kentucky, 2003. Print.

Richards, Donna M. "Let the Circle Be Unbroken." *African Culture: The Rhythms of Unity.* Westport, CT: Greenwood, 1985. Print.

Smitherman, Geneva. *Black Talk: Words and Phrases from the Hood to the Amen Corner.* Boston: Houghton Mifflin, 1994. Print.

Southern, Eileen. *The Music of Black Americans: A History.* New York: Norton, 1983. Print.

Werner, Craig Hansen. *A Change Is Gonna Come: Music, Race, and the Soul of America.* New York: Penguin, 1999. Print.

West, Cornel, and Eddie S. Glaude Jr., eds. *African American Religious Thought: An Anthology.* Louisville, KY: Westminster John Knox, 2003. Print.

Wilson, Sule Greg. *The Drummer's Path: Moving the Spirit with Ritual and Traditional Drumming.* Rochester, VT: Destiny, 1992. Print.

5

OF REBELS, TRICKSTERS, AND SUPERNATURAL BEINGS

Toward a Semiotics of Myth Performance in African Caribbean and Afro-Brazilian Dramas

Dannabang Kuwabong

In this chapter, I engage multiple evaluative processes to uncover and explain the plethora of recurrent tropes and cultural signs and symbols manifested in African Caribbean and Afro-Brazilian dramas. The texts I use for this purpose are Pepe Carril's *Shango de Irma*, Abdias do Nascimento's *Sortilege II: Zumbi Returns*, and Michael Gilkes's *Couvade: A Dream Play of Guyana*. I intend to address African Diasporic dramatic re-creation of West African religious ritual and myth performances, which draw on a repertoire of re-membered historical, cultural, and supernatural tropes and figures and present them onstage in order to construct tentative cohesions of collective consciousness. I postulate that the plays are pivotal to a program of resurrecting, renaming, rezoning, reactivating, and institutionalizing ancient African religious myths in their new locations, to contextualize the deep-rooted desires of African Diaspora peoples for a sense of historical and cultural personhood and belongingness.

In "Mother/Word," the introduction to *Totem Voices: Plays from the Black World Repertory*, Paul Carter Harrison declares unambiguously that "ritual [performance] is the effective technique common to most theatrical exercises of the black world" (xii). In ritual performance words and actions become what he then labels the spirit of "Nommo force" that activates the dramatic mode (context of experience) and reveals the symbolic gestures of the mask (characterization) (xii). Harrison further asserts that "embedded within these modes are references to common experience, myths, and significations that define the collective moral universe" of the African in Diaspora (xii). Performance words and actions that reference and unmask collective myths and moral universe in this sense resemble what Wole Soyinka in *Myth, Literature, and the African World* presents as the metalanguage engaged in myth and ritual performance to reveal "psychic substructure and temporal subsidence, the cumulative history and empirical observations of the community" (1). Following this line of thinking, ritual and myth performance border on the sacred and the religious; the ritualized language and gestures and the use of dance, music, mimesis, and drums, among other performance-enhancing strategies, help transform the dramatic performance into a process of reconciliation of the past, the present, and the future.

Corollary to the statements above, Jay Wright (13) asserts that ritual then must be seen as an enabling tool to unpack historical communal experiences couched in the symbolic language of myth in order to attain that transcendence over quotidian existence among people of the African Diasporas. Here, quotidian existence is founded on the multiple issues of history of slavery, exile, negation, and racism, among other negative effects of their new world experiences. Thus, in myth performance through ritual action, language—both verbal/oral and nonverbal—rises beyond its informational performance and enters into the force field of transformative and transfigurative revelation. Transfigurative revelation is generated in the force field of words, silences, rhythms, movements in dance, drumbeats, and choric responses that weld together to energize the involved image(s) or god(s) or spirit(s) and to unite the actant(s) and participant audience. Subsequently, in African and African Diaspora religious rituals, actions and words are performed audibly or silently. Within the ritual space, the actants, priests/priestesses, ritual/sacred objects, setting, and, most of all, the collective inner desires of the community generate a spirit energy that opens the portals for the descent of the god(s) or spirit(s) to fellowship with humans (Soyinka 145). Soyinka concludes that sacred or secular drama that assembles the same set of paraphernalia or ritual and metalaguage of myth constructs a chain of balances that is both empowering and humbling in its ability to combat negative realities calmly.

Similarly, Victor Leo Walker Jr. posits that "black Africans in the Diaspora . . . create performative rituals . . . to reaffirm the life of the community by engaging the community in an experience that reinforces their collective worldview in which the natural rhythms and the cosmic balances of the community, despite periodic disruptions, are in harmony" (14). Performance ritual then becomes a transcendental and transfigurative maneuver that rises above pure structural religious ceremonies to encompass what Joe C. de Graft calls word, action, and silence. Word, action, and silence, according to de Graft, "enable [humans] to empathize physically, emotionally, and intellectually with the forces that threaten [their] very existence" (21). Through performative rituals, de Graft argues, humans are, at the "deepest levels of consciousness" (21), able to combat psychological disorders caused by traumas of history whether natural or human orchestrated. For instance, for African Diasporic populations living in the Caribbean and South America, dance performance becomes a mythic ritual, a kind of "motive force" (21) that guarantees their unrelenting search for personal and social equilibrium. Performative and performance ritual, whether sacred or secular, provides for these communities' safe psychosomatic and political, spiritual, and cultural spaces in which "participants seek . . . social solidarity, or through which they . . . reaffirm, keep alive, or commemorate . . . facts [of life and historical and cultural] relationships, and attitudes as the community considers vital to their security and continued healthy existence" (23).

Consequently, in African Diaspora dance and drama, through the engagement of ritual performance to re-enact the community's myths, whether of the African past or of their present historical experiences, in which African deities, legends, and other culture heroes/heroines are invoked and evoked, the performers and audience both enter into a spiritualized space of negotiated alliances with the community's remembered cosmogony. Thus, Soyinka observes that the attributes of the deities of the Yoruba pantheon, "in addition to their manipulable histories, have made them the favorites of poets and dramatists, modern and traditional" (1). Further, Soyinka adds that these deities know how to journey, as evident in the African Diaspora "world of the Americas . . . in its socio-religious reality and in the secular arts and literature" (1). Consequently, Soyinka concludes, "symbols of Yemaya (Yemoja), Oxosi (Ososi), Exu (Esu), and Xango (Sango) [Obatala, Ogun, Oshun, among others] . . . are fused with the twentieth-century technological and revolutionary expression of the mural arts of Cuba, Brazil and much of the Caribbean" (1). These deities are often "represented in dramas by the passage-rites of hero-gods," the staged mythopoeic "projection of man's conflict with the forces which challenge his efforts to harmonize with his environment, physical, social and psychic" (1). Babatunde Lawal echoes this in his statement that within African drama, rituals and myths encode "ideas and ideals," and through word and image, performers are able to "mediate between the human and spirit worlds" (41). Hence, memory as cosmic DNA among African Caribbean and Afro-Brazilian communities must be seen as race dramas representing race memory. Thus, "race drama," writes Alan Locke, functions as the supplier of "imaginative channel[s] of escape and spiritual release, and then by some process of emotional reinforcement to cover life with the illusion of . . . spiritual freedom" (iv).

Clayton Riley's argument that *Sortilege II: Zumbi Returns* by Abdias do Nascimento of Brazil expresses the "collective psychic [physiognomic and historical] energies" of Afro-Brazilians is also applicable to *Couvade* by Michael Gilkes of Guyana and to *Shango de Irma* by Pepe Carril of Cuba. These plays therefore can be said to reflect Paul Carter Harrison's idea that African and African Diaspora myth performances in the form of ritual drama are like spiritual clearinghouses "where the collected energies of Black people coalesce to define their own peculiar" humanity amid an environment of self-imposed negrophobia (196). These clearinghouses enable Africans in Diaspora to deal with what Edouard Glissant sees as the trauma of truncated histories which generates chasms that frustrate connectivity or relations with their African roots. I argue that these plays engage performative rituals to recreate myths of origins and charter new paths through which links can be re-generated with Africa and with themselves as a community. The three plays engage mythologies of Yoruba deities and the ritual performances associated with those myths to reveal the role of African deities in the lives of Diaspora Africans. The remembered rituals, according to Edouard Glissant, are therefore "the armature that frames the god, even the rite that surrenders it to a final pyre, the god assembled cane by cane, reed by reed, line by line" toward a "restoration of [their] shattered histories, [their] shards of vocabulary" (66–67).

The three plays in this chapter range in complexity and purported agendas. However, they all relate to the deepest desires of African Diaspora peoples of Cuba, Guyana, and Brazil to rekindle their spiritual and mythological connection with an Africa of their ancestors denied them in the cauldron of their traumatic historical experiences. In these dramatized myths of African reconnections, the plays' ideological thrusts seek to re-establish and re-present onstage their concepts of origins, meanings, beliefs, customs, histories, and human relationships, and thus they all embody, in symbolic language, systematized values that frame and "phrase the philosophy underlying" their "culture from all others as a way of life" (Herskovitz and Herskovitz 81–82). Through their dramas, Nascimento, Giles, and Carril all then engage myth performance through drama and dance to help transform African Diaspora peoples who otherwise may be living merely for what Campbell calls bodily ends so that they begin to live for cultural and spiritual ends (38).

But what is the difference between performance ritual and ritual performance in the context of drama and dance? Performance ritual assumes that narratives can be staged or performed according to certain laid-down sets of rites and/or regulations. Thus, in sacred rites, there are formulaic, standardized sets of actions across generations that determine the authenticity of the ritual performed. The reenactments of these rites or steps in ritual then give rise to the idea of ritual performance. In a way, the two are inseparable, though one may know the necessary steps needed to perform a ritual without performing it. But one cannot perform a ritual if one has not mastered the accepted procedural apparatuses unless, of course, the ritual is in the process of gestation. As mentioned above, ritual performance encapsulates a mythopoeic narrative that conjures up race/tribe/community memory. Consequently, for my argument, race memory in relation to the three plays in this study echoes the idea of Nommo force or what has been popularized as *asé, axé, atse,* that force Robert Farris Thompson sees as the spirit force of the gods that inhabit Afro-Cuban sacred art (5–9). Thus, to Henry John Drewal et al. (1989), *asé* is that life-giving force which enables African Diaspora people to create songs, praises, drama, prayers, curses, poetry, dance, sculpture, oratory, and ritual in order to seek amelioration of the disruption and breakage of their organic roots in the cultural soils of Africa. Through *asé* or Nommo force, ritual performance, whether sacred or secular, is a re-generative dramatic/theatrical system for new beginnings and new transformations. Similarly, Soyinka sees the idea of "space, music, poetry or material paraphernalia in the drama . . . [as a] move directly from the apparent to deeper effects with the community whose drama (that is history, morality, affirmation, supplication, thanksgiving . . .) it also is" (145).

In making this argument, I am aware of the uniforming, sensational, exoticized, and commoditized performance antics in several African Diaspora dances and dramas purporting to recreate authentic African ritual drama and dance onstage (Harrison, "Mother/Word" xxxviii), the type Walcott sneers at in his critiques of exoticism as Afrocentric art ("What the Twilight Says: An Overture"). It is this type of hollow ritual performance in the African Diaspora that Aimé Cesairé's Rebel in *And the Dogs Were Silent* rejects as impotent and of no salvific value in the struggle of the slave from death of culture and soul. In these rituals, the African gods refuse to answer and act, and thus he declares them dead in the new environment. Similarly, these African deities, remembered only in name but not in substance, are rejected by Walcott's Makak in *Dream on Monkey Mountain* in his rejection of the temptation to be a new world African Moses, though the potential for spiritual, cultural, and racial revival and liberation from death by whiteness is suggested in his healing ritual of Josephus effected within Spiritual Baptist's prayer performance.

Both Césaire's and Walcott's antiheroes reject an Afrocentric predilection to privilege negritude because it is ill defined and puerile, and because their locations in Martinique and St. Lucia/Trinidad speak more of deeper cultural deracination than Nascimento's hero whose history is resplendent with cultural, political, and spiritual resistance in Brazil's Quilombos. Thus, Emanuel in *Sortilege II: Zumbi Returns* stands at the crossroads of redemption through re-enacting ritual sacrifice to presage his journey back to an Afro-Brazilian self. *Sortilege II: Zumbi Returns* is in a way also linked to Giles's *Couvade*, where the hero is given the cloak of redemption through art from inspiration received in dreamtime. My objective in this study, then, is to show how through these dramas as ritual performances, African mythologies that crossed the Atlantic are re-articulated on stage and re-instated (Drewal 1–135) in their right places to oppose what Harrison sees as their trivialization and commoditization by the dominant Euro-American cultures, whether in North America, the Caribbean, or South America, for an entertainment industry designed and controlled by Euro-American industrial conglomerates. He writes: "no matter how we decorate the African persona, the creative impulse invariably reflects race memory, which should not be construed as nostalgia or sentimental atavism" ("Mother/Word" xxxviii). Thus, where the dramatized reproduction on stage of these myths and rituals lacks revelatory illumination and transformative direction in the lives of African Diaspora peoples, it becomes a newer, more insidious form of self-mockery (xli).

Harrison, like Edouard Glissant (66–67), does not deny cultural and geographical particularities; nonetheless, he stresses that what unites Black people of African descent globally are their shared histories of the transatlantic slave trade conducted by a Christian Europe. The three plays under discussion in this chapter—*Shango de Irma, Couvade*, and *Sortilege II: Zumbi Returns*—all open with sacred music accompanied by the sacred drum to create the appropriate ritual clearing in which space, time, action, history, and community coalesce and facilitate the performance of memorized historical experiences. In the opening scene of *Shango de Irma*, the use of Yoruba esoteric religious music, objects of worship, and Obatala's narrative of her beginnings and historical roles in Yoruba culture as an androgynous goddess, as well as her transatlantic journey with slaves of Yoruba descent to the Americas, especially to Cuba and Brazil, are given as a testimony of remembrance and hope to the descendants of Africa in the Americas. In addition, the opening of *Shango de Irma* with drums and music becomes instrumental in securing what Harrison describes as "communal participation in both sacred and secular ceremonies" ("Mother/Word" xxxiv). Harrison's observation is derived from W. E. Abraham's interpretation of Akan culture where he talks of the "need to adapt musical trials to the proceedings without submerging the verbal account forced here raconteur to seek musical qualities in . . . words." Thus, the engagement of music and drums, argues Nathaniel McKay, becomes and recognizes that music (both verbal and instrumental) is the "phantom limb that arises from [its] capacity for feeling." He notes: "Phantom is a relativizing term which cuts both ways, occasioning a shift in perceptive between real and unreal, an exchange of attributes between the two" (34). These observations become more urgent in *Shango de Irma* and *Sortilege II: Zumbi Returns*.

The use of song, dance, and drum to alter perspective through the destabilization of time and space is initialized and maintained in the ritualized sacred language performed by voice, chorus, and drums, which creates a sacred space/stage for "Obatala, mother of earth and of man, of justice and of purity" (Carril 48) to manifest herself/himself.

> Voice, chorus, and drums:
> Barasuayo . . .

a moni ara guana
ma ma quena iraguo e
Barasuayo . . .
. . .
O barasuayo
e . . . kee . . .
Echwodura
o moni ara guana
mama quera iraguo e . . .
(The illuminated altar of Obatala appears, carried by her children.)
Voice, chorus and drums:
Enn aye mimoslieo
enu aye mi baba (repeat)
Obatala ta wini wini
se e icelpre
bobo la ina fere . . . (repeat)

"The drums . . . call the orishas to descend and join the fiesta" (Murphy 93). The incantatory device engaged here, rather than retarding narrative progression, becomes in its insistent tone an unrelenting, invigorating catalyst that splits the wall dividing the worlds of common human reality and mythic reality. Through this fissuring between the spirit world and the material world, the world of dreams and reality merge into dream reality, and the performers and audience are both transported momentarily into a world of convergence where possibilities are etched and hope delivered against historical and socioeconomic and political contradictions. According to the stage directions, the song is an invocation of Elegua (Elegba), god of crossroads, the trickster god whose capriciousness enable us to see multiple sides of things, while dissolving differences as we recognize those differences are caused by perceptual positions. The invocation of Elegba (Elegua) to initiate the ceremony in itself reconnects the actions and narrative performances and rituals among African Diaspora communities of believers with African continental believers and, subsequently, erases the new historical, geographical, and linguistic distances caused by the historical realities of the transatlantic slave trade. Joseph Murphy records a Santeria adherent who confirms that the opening drum music means "They are asking Eleggua to open the way for us. . . . If you don't ask Eleggua first he may become insulted and he won't open up the gate for the rest of the orishas" (94).

The invocation of Eleggua and Obatala also signifies a movement toward merging different roads at the center. In the center of the cross-roads, remembrance and narrative performance of old myths provides the possibility of closure for old pains and openings for new possibilities for coping. The invocation of Elegua, the "mediator and operator of doors" (Murphy 47) is a significant ritual that situates the play's dynamic at the crossroads of African Diaspora peoples. Crossroads in their migration and exile experience what can be engaged to set new visions and paths of growth in the environments and realities if not a call to a return to a physical topos called Africa, because Africa is in them in the new place. Invocation is not merely a ritualized action designed to prepare a hallowed ground so that the devotee can experience the presences of the gods and commune with them for guidance, but it also entails a set of guided prayers that confirms the devotee's vision, hearing, and feeling of the presence of the gods as they re-perform narratives of re-birthing and re-journeying toward the valley of hope (Murphy 93). Thus, Obatala, the androgynous god/dess, king/queen, mother-father, and so on, opens the performance with a self-introduction in which her role and powers are itemized. As a god she/he is constantly metamorphosing though remaining constant, unlike the Jewish/Hindu/Buddhist/Christian/Islamic gods that have stopped growing:

> Obatala: I, Orishanla, am born of Olodumare, Uan Mariqueno, Olofi made father and mother of the sky and of earth. I was always sanctified and old. I was never able to be child, to live the life of an ordinary woman. . . . But I have my sixteen roads. I have humility. I am loving, vengeful, voluptuous, and simple. I am father, mother, king, and queen. I am wise and serene. I am the mistress of destiny. (She laughs). And I am also nothing.
> . . . I have the power of all minds, and I bring retribution to those whose minds are evil. (*Shango de Irma* 48–49)

Obatala's testament is not focused on her powers, but on her mission across the oceans. Here is also the play's rhetorical ideology. Africans did not arrive here godless. They may have arrived naked physically, but they carried their spirituality and religions in their hearts and heads, in their music and cultures, their drums and deuces. Thus, Obatala confides in us the following historical facts that border on a new mythology: "There came a time when it was necessary for me to cross the waters. The dark and turbulent waters that warned me of death. I don't know if it was a fear of death or if it was the terror of submerging myself in the solitary house of the water, but I begged Agayu to let me cross in his boat" (49).

In this narrative of transatlantic watery crossing, the focus is not on Obatala's androgynous nature but on her ability to shape-shift from woman to man, and to a bird of peace. It is this bird of peace and Obatala's other qualities, such as wisdom, strategic changeability, forgiveness, and vision, that the devotees seek in order to survive and prosper in their new location. Thus, the ritual of recall itself is not the salient point in this play even if it initiates the beginnings of the search for identity in *Shango de Irma*. The journey of Obatala, double in its signification (journey from the world of gods to that of humans over the watery turbulence and journey from West Africa to the Caribbean in the slave boats or indenture boats), provides us the background against which Shango's (Africans in Diaspora) new world identity can be defined, described, understood, and celebrated. But for this to become a reality, Shango must navigate through a labyrinth of misleading paths toward the center of the crossroads from which his true identity springs. Thus, when Shango asks his mother a series of questions— "mother, I want to know my name" (50), "I also want to know your name, so that I can know where I come from" (51), and "I want to know the name of my father" (51)—he is asking the perennial question asked by African Caribbean people: Who are we? To know one's own name, one's ancestral origins, and one's maternal and paternal names is to know oneself. So far, as the play testifies, the African Caribbean does not yet know these and hence lives a vicarious life of self-unknowing. Rather than deny or answer Shango's requests, Obatala avoids the issue. Nonetheless, after she tells him the name of the biological father, she encourages the inquisitive Shango to undertake the traditional mythical hero's journey of self-knowledge to seek out his own meaning in life. But to the question of what his name is, Shango is given an answer that is pregnant with many possibilities. Obatala tells Shango: "[C]all yourself anything you please. There are as many names for a man as there are pebbles in a mountain" (50).

The search by Shango for his biological father, Agayu—a search to claim his patrilineality—becomes a symbolic and mystical journey of return to an Africa of mythical imagination, cultural reclaiming, and new beginnings (M. T. Drewal 29–62), a search that involves a transfigurative journey through fire, the opposite element of water (55–60) that Obatala transversed on her journey to his birth and naming in the new world of the Americas. Finding the father and trying to claim filiation with Agayu is both mythical and historical. Mythical in the sense of the origins of Shango's progress from a child devoid of powers to a deity in the making; historical because it is linked to the deep desire of the children of African descent in the Caribbean, whose ancestors arrived in the slave ships, to rediscover and reclaim their African roots, their spiritualities, cultures, and personhoods. But the search itself is laced with the danger of death. Death, however, represented by Iku (52–54), must hold no absolute dominion over the children of Africa represented by Shango. It is hence pertinent to note that death unwittingly plays a role of initiating and establishing the ground rules for the ritual that leads to transfiguration of Shango from a powerless boy to a man with the power over death. Death is symbolic of the loss of identity, and the ritual that gives Shango back life that is now immortal is a mythic metaphor that gives hope to African Caribbean peoples of a new resurrection that will transform them from a helpless people to a mighty people in the new world. The story of Shango is their story. But this does not go without problems. For instance, in scenes 4 and 7 in which Agayu tries to deny his son, we encounter the problematic attempt to return and claim citizenship of African Diasporic peoples, especially those descended from the transatlantic slave trade. Their return becomes a journey of baptism by death, baptism by fire, and a resurrection in which Shango's physical body, having been destroyed, becomes a spiritual body that no longer obeys the rule of the elements.

> Shango: The fire has charred my skin,
> but I'm not really wounded,
> Father. If you were to destroy
> me, it would matter to me,
> because you are my father. (58)

Shango's transfiguration from a half-mortal to a deity is facilitated by a trinitarian coalition of Oya, Oshun, and Olofi. Oshun's protection ensures Shango a "better path" (59) in life, and Oya's gift of illumination ensures Shango "will arrive formally in the heavens of Olofi" (59). It is thus at the hands of the African gods that the children of African Diaspora are ensured a better path, illumination, and final arrival in a home of heartsease. The implication is this: those who desire complete transformation must seek this through a baptism of fire, suffering but guided and protected by their faith and submission to the gods and their African ancestors. Any other path leads to perdition and white death by Iku. The search cannot be half-hearted but must be persistent as shown by the boy Shango.

> Shango: Mother, I have returned to you
> And to my home, and I content.
> I have satisfied my desire for knowledge.
> I am the happiest of men. I have been close to my father. (61)

In this search, which includes the ritual of purification and resurrection by fire and transfiguration, Shango rejects the negative and life-in-death encounter he has with his father and translates the treatment by his father: denial, murder, and incineration is a good thing because out of it all, he is deified. Had Agayu not treated him thus, Shango would never have risen to godhead status. Thus, the trauma at the hands of his father becomes a cleansing, a preparation for the gift of fire, lightning, thunder. Following this logic of thought, it is rational to conclude that Shango's story becomes a testimony of hope for the children of Africa, who like Shango have suffered the cruelties of slavery, racism, and dehumanization, yet have come out of them all a stronger people, both spiritually and psychosomatically.

To the question, "Why didn't you stay with him then" (61), a question often posed to those who in the African Diaspora acclaim the preeminence of African cultures, religions, civilizations, and history, asking why they do not then pack and leave for Africa, a philosophy preached by Marcus Garvey, Shango responds: "I wanted to come and give you the news. My father taught me many things. Look . . . the fire is now my natural element" (61). But his enthusiasm does not enthrall Obatala; she assaults him and evicts him. How do we read this action by Obatala? Are Agayu's and Obatala's actions to be read as an indictment of African Caribbean people who seek to define their personhoods through an Afrocentric ideology and spirituality by indicating that the re-duplication of African gods in the new world leads to another rejection from the African side? Are Walcott and Aimé Césaire not then justified when they write that the African gods are dead in the Caribbean and their invocation on stage is useless romanticism and exoticization? I ask these questions because the rest of *Shango de Irma* is a dramatization of the journey of Shango to godhead. There is the mythical path to godhead through many dangerous paths: war with Agayu, Iku, and Ogun; caught between the rivalry between Oshun and Oya; and finally caught in an incestuous relationship with his stepmother, Yemaya. The penalty for the crimes Shango is said to have committed is given with a spirit of resilience and hope. Obatala, who opens the play, ends it in these words to Shango, and by association to Afro-Cubanos:

> Obatala: And this compliance will be your punishment, Shango de Irma. The joy which makes suffering possible, the birth which leads to death will be your punishment and the punishment of all men. . . . You are, by the designation of Olofi, eternal keeper of fire. . . . If the eyes of your sons, your lights, become extinguished, light them again if you can, Shango de Irma, *orishas* of the flames, and see them extinguished again and again in the eternal cycle which follows your battles without end. (89)

Thus, the play ends with a gift of a spirit of eternal renewal. This spirit given to Shango, rather than being seen as a gift that fails to promise a life of eternal rest and peace in a place far removed from the reality of human existence, must be seen as a gift known in Yoruba spirituality as *Ase.* Shango is given the gift of fire from all sources; that fire is the spirit force that animates all material things and humans also. Shango is given the responsibility through his devotees to give hope to those in despair and those who are lost in the cauldron of history. Thus, the play also demonstrates the sources of African Caribbean people's resilience and hope.

Esiala Irobi, in "In the Theory of Ase: The Persistence of African Performance Aesthetics in the North American Diaspora—August Wilson, Ntozake Shange and Djanet Sears," engages Yoruba cosmogony to read African Diaspora modes of thought and action, especially how the cultural performances they create to define their particular ethos and mythos differ remarkably in essence from the Judeo-Christian Euro-American cultural and spiritual modes of performance, drama, myth, and art. Though the concept and theory of *Ase* (*Atse*) is not new to Yoruba people, or for that matter African peoples, its development and subsequent appropriation as a viable cultural praxis to read the works of Africa and its Diaspora was publically launched by Robert Farris Thompson in his 1984 descriptive analysis of Afro-Cuban Diaspora spiritual artifacts. Irobi's position is that the ignorance of African cultural and performance theory and practice in Western academia was caused by a lack of understanding of the role played by orality and performance in the development of theory in African cultures. Because there were no written texts to dig into, it was thought that theory per se could never exist in African cultural praxes. In Thompson's mind, *Ase,* as understood in Afro-Cuban art, is the spirit force that the creator imbues in humans, a force that can be used for good or evil. This idea is further explored by Henry John Drewal and Drewal et al. They argue that *Ase* is that life-generating spirit that gives songs, praises, prayers, curses, poetry, sculpture, oratory, drama, and ritual, among others, the power of recreation and transformation. But for this to manifest, there must be a regenerative system in the Diaspora community to ensure their continuous and continual survival and growth.

Thus, as postulated and argued by numerous theorists on African Diaspora performances and theatre, theatre community is the overriding ideal soil and drive of African and African Diaspora imagery (Harrison 76). Theatre is "an art of community by which a given group ritualizes and perpetuates its sense of identity, its values, history, performance, aesthetics and the use of spirituality as a basis for continuity" (16). Similarly, in *African Theatre and Modern Drama*, Kacke Götrick sees African drama as a complex of presentational and representational performances revealing efficaciousness, "conceived of as a duality by the approximate spectators, comprising reality and fiction simultaneously" (123–33). Of course, the whole issue of duality undermines the otherwise visionary reading. I would argue for a reading that goes beyond a simplistic tendency to see things in duality toward a vision of reading that calls for a multiplicity of perceiving and understanding through the processes of complicated relationship among actors, on the one hand, and audiences, on the other hand, who not only watch but also participate in the acting, and the nonmaterial equivalences of the two- and three-dimensional historical times of the past, present, and future. And for the African Diasporas, these relationships become more complicated yet more exhilarating. First, there is the multiplication of the three dimensions into six: There are the original African roots of the past, then the adaptation of those roots in foreign soil and circumstances, the African present and presence of which becomes transmuted within a creolized present/presence and synthesized with other cultures through the forces of translocation and transculturation. The future still looks to the African past and present yet must diverge toward a creation of a new path of their future that runs in continuous parallel to the future of those in Africa. But what ultimately unites the world of African Diasporas is what Irobi defines as the holistic, an inseparable synthesis of the mythopoeic, aesthetic, and ritual. This spirit force is evoked through dance, music, and sacerdotal language. Thus, in *Shango de Irma* we find an abundant use of dance, music, and poetry. These three elements are necessary ingredients in the creation of a mystical atmosphere that can then induce possession by the gods. Joseph Murphy in *Santería: An African Religion in America*, Miguel F. Santiago in *Dancing with the Saints*, and others have written copiously about the powerful role of music, dance, and esoteric language of prayer and invocation in African-derived religions in the Americas. It is *Ase* therefore that Abdias do Nascimento celebrates in his play *Sortilege II: Zumbi Returns.*

Sortilege II: Zumbi Returns engages ritual and performance tools including membranophones, wind instruments, altars, paints, and war instruments, assembling them to initiate the ritual that opens dream portals linking Diaspora Africans to their origins of existence. For instance, in the opening scene we are transported and transplanted into natural ecological settings in which the dense tropical forest clearings in the interior landscapes of Brazil are both symbolic representations of the inner spaces of Diaspora Africans and also representations of the need for rootedness and connectivity with nature, the source of origin and spiritual forces. The naturalistic settings reveal the playwright's desire to remove the ceremonies of ritual reincarnation far away from the corruptions and distractions of city life, and to seek connectivity with the spirituality of nature. In these natural surroundings, nature then provides a sanctified space for the ritual of initiation to usher the participants into time past, present, and future. The selected clearing in the forests also calls for a journey into the inner recesses of being of Diaspora Africans to examine their lives and seek a healing. These inner places become necessary as they provide that welcome space for the gods, Nommo force, or spirits to enter in dialogue with humans. The sites also give the ritual a greater atmosphere of magic, a necessary ingredient in ritual and myth performance. These locational maneuvers undermine objections raised by cultural purists in both the African and African Diasporic worlds, which Soyinka critiques as mere abstractions (5). He argues that the issue of territorial, cultural, historical, and spiritual truncation raised by these purists is problematically delimiting, and he questions whether in reality, "the emotive progression which leads to a communal ecstasy has been destroyed in the process of re-staging" (7). Interestingly, the selected playwrights preempt this criticism by creating new symbolic patches of earth in naturalistic settings and thereby manage to stage the paths to redemption or rites of passage of the deity/hero away from the profanity of the common gaze, while simultaneously ensuring framing of the dramas along what Soyinka calls "racial and social constructs" (8).

Sortilege II: Zumbi Returns is a mythical, more spiritually complicated, and ritualized reclamatory performance of the 1957 *Sartilegio* (*Mysterious Negro*). It is a response to the deep desire of Afro-Brazilians to engage in re-conserving and articulating their African cultural and cosmic worlds toward de-blanching their history and culture and ensuring that the African contribution to Brazilian European culture is recognized and accepted as central to Brazilian culture. As the author argues eloquently in the introduction, the idea in *Sortilege* is "to ransom the dignity of the Black [people] and [their] culture, to verify and proclaim Black beauty from its essential core, to consider its intricate value as its only foundation and parameter" (Introduction to *Sartilegio* [*Black Mystery*]). The play by Nascimento, according to Elisa Larkin Nascimento, exposes and challenges what she calls Brazil's negrophobia ideology couched as "racial democracy" that culturally, legally, politically, and historically denies the existence and contribution of Afro-Brazilians. *Sortilege* dramatizes the myth of racial equality with the whitewash of racial democracy (204).

The history of the play's journey from conception to performance to print and revision to its present form testifies to the illusion of "racial democracy" in Brazil and indeed in Latin American nations, where discussions about race/ethnicity are always dismissed under the rubric of national identity. Censored and banned for six years from 1951 to 1957 by the Brazilian race-and-thought police as subversive to the ideological processing of people of African descent into the stranglehold of Europeanization, the play first saw the light of day in 1957 when it was allowed in theatres as a product of the Teatro Experimental do Negro (PEN) founded by the author in 1944. Thomas E. Skidmore has ably documented this official policy of whitening Brazil in the first part of the twentieth century in *Black into White: Race and Nationality in Brazilian Thought*.

Sortilege II: Zumbi Returns is a celebration in many ways of the histories of African presence, resistance, and survival in South America and the Caribbean. It takes as its compass real history that records the maroon kingdoms across Latin America and the Hispanic Caribbean. Known as Quilombo in Brazil, these maroon nations were also called *cumbes* in Colombia, and in Venezuela, Cuba, and other Caribbean territories they were known as *palenques*. Set in the jungles or on top of inaccessible mountains, these communities fought off repossession by the mercenary armies of Europe. The history of Black Caribs of St. Vincent, Honduras, and Dominica also testify to how well these communes were organized and how they thrived and flourished on African concepts of politics, economics, and spirituality. *Sortilege* celebrates Zumbi, the last democratically elected king, and the Palmares community in Brazil, and how the community successfully resisted several attempts from 1595 to 1696 to re-conquer them. Zumbi and his Palmares community's history have now entered into Afro-Brazilian cultural mythology, and the play performs this history. Elisa Larkin Nascimento argues that "*Sortilege . . .* engages the basic elements of Afro-Brazilian religious culture to question the ingrained alienation expressed in [Afro-Brazilian's] own efforts to whiten themselves on the inside, culturally and psychologically, having internalized the dominant white [Brazilian] society's cultural norms" (204). Thus, what Fanon examines in *Black Skin, White Masks*, Walcott explores in *Dream on Monkey Mountain*, and Trevor Rhone identifies in *Old Story Time* is shared by Nascimento. But while these others focus more on materialist paradigms and the African Diaspora characters do not seriously examine the paths to real racial, cultural, and spiritual liberation, Nascimento's play seriously engages the political, racial, religious, and cultural to that end.

For instance, Aimé Césaire, in spite of his Negritudinist politics in *Return to My Native Land* and *Discourse on Colonialism*, rejects African spirituality in plays such as *And the Dogs Were Silent*, *The Tragedy of King Chistophe*, and *A Season in the Congo* and argues only for Marxist revolution. Similarly, Walcott's *Dream on Monkey Mountain* and *Henri Christophe* beat hasty retreats from fully engaging African-based spirituality as a strategic ally in the fight for cultural liberation from the negating hold Eurocentricism has on African Caribbeans. Even in Rhone's play, which seems to examine the power of African-derived beliefs in Jamaica, only the negative aspects are used to try to break up a purely materialist and undeveloped Black consciousness. There are other plays, such as *Shango de Irma* and Zora Zeljan's *Oxala*, in the Caribbean and

Brazil that stage the dramas of Yoruba deities without actually demonstrating how this spirituality can be a liberating, enabling, and creative force, *axé*, for racial and cultural regeneration. Elisa Larkin Nascimento identifies three basic concepts that shape and inform the actions and events in *Sortilege*: *axé*, *dispatch*, and *spiritual possession*:

> *Axé* is the basic life force which moves the cosmos in its different realms. Without axé, there is no life, and life is the central concern of African religion. Thus the basic purpose of religious practice is to ensure the perpetuation and reproduction of *axé*, and its transmission in order to preserve the harmonious balance of energies among different cosmic realms. This is the function of the *dispatch*, or sacrificial offering . . . in order to restore balance where cosmic harmony has been disturbed. . . .
>
> Spiritual possession is another expression of this concept of transmission of *axé*, in which an entity from another cosmic realm—*Orixa* or an ancestor—visits the human community of worshippers. The entity converses and interacts with those present, increasing their *axé* by giving counsel, reinforcing faith, and guiding people in difficult decisions (205).

Tempting as the pull toward a spiritualized reading of the play is, I will not venture there, as the author himself warns that the spirituality must not be allowed to obfuscate or interfere with the dramaturgy or performance of the play as a secular piece. The problem, however, in this kind of drama is to recognize the borders between sacred and secular performances that engage the same rituals, icons, narratives, metalaguage, and acoustics on stage. It is a fact that in both African and Afro-Brazilian societies, there is often a blurred distinction in the cosmic excursions of spiritual forces and the material world:

> The Candomblé, or Macumba, ceremony is an integral part of the "mystery." But it must not interfere with the play's action or prejudice the atmosphere of magic and unreality crucial to the revolution and the hero's real and intimate drama. Indeed, a naturalistic transportation of Afro-Brazilian religious ceremony would only mar the play, which does not intend to bring to the stage an ethnographic picture of Macumba or Candomblé, nor simply a folkloric display of African rites. (206)

Nascimento's prescription and proscription here testify to the slippery slopes encountered by African Diaspora playwrights when seeking to create representational African-centered arts without exoticization. *Sortilege II: Zumbi Returns* displays, more than any other African Diasporic play, all the performance elements that inform a well-researched and passionately constructed play in which ritual, myth, history, language, and magic are carefully synchronized and synthesized to give a drama of spiritual realism. The performance realm is both magical and realistic, as the stage is a form of worship/devotional space. The forest setting echoes the historical location of the Palmares community, set apart to enable them to resurrect and perform their history and culture through religious rites. The sacred nature of the setting is emphasized by the visible presence of an altar/tomb that signals a ritual performance of sacrificial death and continuity among ancestral presences. Thus, the ritual paraphernalia for a Macumba ceremony is staged for political reasons and resonates with a spirituality that is invoked toward that end. Subsequently, the atmosphere is charged with a realism that is at once magical and expectational: "It is essential throughout the play to bring out the unreal nature of the temporal and spatial setting" (207). Hence, the stage directions at this point are painstakingly elaborate and detailed so as to engage our total participation as we see character impersonations of Oshun, Ogun, and Shango / Eshu Elegbara. There is an ethereal presence in the forest clearing as all the sacred objects of a religious ceremony are present and the call of the dogs at night, a symbolic echo of the power of songs to see, hear, smell, and feel unseen presences at night, what humans cannot see. The seating arrangement in which the Iyalorixa or Babalorixa are surrounded by the Filhas de Santos demonstrates how in this play Nascimento advocates that the path to Afro-Brazilian cultural liberation must be somehow centered around the five centuries of resilience provided in the Afro-Brazilian religion of Candomblé, or Macumba, as the priest invites the devotees to their ancient yet contemporary African spiritual nexus.

Thus, the barking of dogs signals the exact temporal appropriateness for action to commence. The language of ritual that is spoken by Iyalorixa is potent with symbolic imagery. It explains, yet it also confounds. But words alone are incapable of capturing the essence of things, the meaning of existence, of time and memory. Thus, she counsels her neophytes when they ask: "our future . . . ties to our past?" (208) to which her response is: "Try to understand what is beyond things . . . in front of what

I say. Sometimes words betray us. Never trust words; Exu knows the language of humans and of gods . . . ask him. Who can touch the root of words hidden in the depths of spoken mystery" (208). To enter into the mythical and metaphysical worlds of the sacred, the "founding word" must be explored for its "secret of meanings" (208) through the stories of the gods. Thus, to achieve liberation Afro-Brazilians must enter into the world of Afro-Brazilian spirituality, must expiate through sacrifice the numbing European worldview that dominates their lives, even in Afro-Brazilian religions that have been sanctioned by the Catholic Church and appropriated by white Brazilians. One must be able through Afro-Brazilian religious experience to enter the many doors of liberation journeys opened by the *Òrìṣà*.

In *Sortilege II: Zumbi Returns*, the visions of Iyalorixa use words to transverse the oceans of time and space and to link Brazil to Nigeria. But words alone in this performance ritual lack the power to transmit the message and messenger to the ancient mythical-and-yet-present cosmic reality. Thus, many of the objects of ceremony—palm oil, cassava flour, rum, and cigar—are gifts of thanksgiving and negotiation with the gods, and the most powerful symbolic object—an unblemished black rooster, a symbolic rooster whose life is shed—nonetheless becomes the carrier of the message of distress. This portion of the ritual is described as the *dispatch* stage. Soon after, the stage is given to the Filhas de Santos who engage in prophecies of both condemnation and salvation for Emanuel, a doctor of law who lives the life of Fanon's stereotypical Black male in Diaspora, theorized in *Black Skin, White Masks* where Fanon asks, "What Does the Black Male Want?" In the barrage of voices of lamentation, Black females are also interrogated for their imprudence in seeking sexual liaisons with white men.

In this ritual performance, the prophetic appearance of Emanuel shows the efficacy of the *dispatch*; Emanuel has been struck with a madness of identity crisis that causes him to seek leadership through a disparate rush to the sacred spaces of his African Brazilian ancestors. Prior to this moment, Emanuel is under the illusion that because of his Eurocentric education and marriage to Margarida, a white Brazilian woman, he is accepted as an honorary white and hence as an equal to Euro-Brazilians in the lie of racial democracy. His education and marriage to Margarida makes him scornfully abusive toward his African roots. Emanuel denigrates the religion, asserting that African spirituality is a lot of bunk (212).

> Emanuel: They're calling Obatala, to them the greatest of gods. Then comes Xango, Oya, Omolu, Yemanja. . . . Too many gods for only one eternity. . . . Exu is a bad dude. Soon he hears the clock strike midnight he goes out after cigars and rum. (*Thoughtful.*) Think of that. . . . Me, talking like I believed in all this nonsense too. Me, Doctor Emanuel, Esquire, educated Negro, law school graduate, Ph.D., trained attorney . . . baptized and confirmed in Church. (214)

Emanuel's psychosis stems from his repression and rejection of his Afro-Brazilian religion, roots, and people, and this makes him refer to the culture in the most racist terms possible: "animistic cults, evoking savage gods. Gods! As if you could call that gods, that thing that comes onto those stupid niggers. . . . It's nothing more than collective hysteria . . . they worship the saints and the devil at the same time. Exu is the fallen angel, the *macumbeiros'* rebellious angel" (212). Consequently, the madness is both personal and representational of the type of psychosis endured by Afro-Brazilians through the shock therapies of centuries of racism and police brutality against them in the favelas (219). His confused state is exacerbated by a confession to the Othello, Bigger Thomas Syndrome (219).

Though terrified by the pull of what he has tried to erase from his mind and soul, his speech shows a gradual opening of his memory to his childhood, to his mother, and, by association, to a lifting of the veil of whiteness that will finally usher him into the dark light of his soul and mind and reveal to him the path of salvation through sacrifice of his white mask through death. It is this gradual connection of the reality and potent truth of the culture he has tried to discard that holds him back and prevents him from escaping. He is frightened, confused, yet attentively attracted to merge back into something that never left him: his history, spirituality, culture, and personhood. The use of lullabies transfigures the silent traffic legalism of Emanuel into childhood innocence and trauma that must re-live, then be purified and sanctified in preparation for the pivotal role his name suggests he must play in order to become a culture hero of his people.

In this translation down memory lane, a descent into a personal purgatory, Emanuel takes center stage in the ritual performance and lights the incense to create the smoky atmosphere that becomes the gateway to a vision of Ifigenia, the Black woman he loves but rejects in favor of a blond Margarida and the chance to claim himself as social equal with whites. Emanuel's first sign of descent into purgatorial psychosis comes when he becomes the voice of lamentation and bitterness of disillusion in the prison of the Euro-Brazilian world he has so carefully struggled for and gained partial entry into (220–21). The agony of sudden awakening makes him dizzy: "my head is spinning. I'm dizzy, dizzy . . . hearing all these strange noises . . . weirder voices . . . where are all these voices coming from? Forgotten songs . . . lacerated love" (222). From here, the play becomes a litany of voices, an Afro-Brazilian litany of the historical iniquities Africans in Diaspora have suffered at the hands of European peoples in the Americas (224). For even when Emanuel has attained the highest qualifications in the Euro-Brazilian legal system, his dark pigment denies him full entry and equal treatment in Brazilian law (226–27). The recall of this traumatic experience when he tries to defend Ifigenia, who is raped by her white employer, shows how far an Afro-Brazilian is tolerated by the dominant Euro-Brazilian social, economic, legal, and political systems. Remembering these experiences helps Emanuel question his own attitudes toward Afro-Brazilian culture and engage in the process of questioning that follows the moments of transformative clarity acknowledged by an unwilling mind.

But in order to enter fully into this transformative clarity of vision, he first has to experience spiritual possession. The first movement toward this is when Emanuel recalls a near-lynching scene: he is with Margarida; they are kissing and a group of whites finds them, accuses him of sexually assaulting a white girl, beats him to a pulp, and takes him away (225–26). This vision is made possible through trance-like dance movements performed by the Òrìṣà through the use of sacred objects:

> Enter the orixa; who puts resin in the incense burner and blesses Emanuel with smoke. Then he dances a few movements, and without touching Emanuel's body, executes the ceremonial greeting, pretending to touch Emanuel's right shoulder with his own, then repeating with the left shoulder. Then he takes off from his neck an impressive necklace of iron pieces in various shapes. Ogun's guia or ceremonial necklace. He puts it around Emanuel's neck. Emanuel is in a kind of trance, and for some moments dances, following the steps that the Orixa continues to perform. (226)

All this takes place while there is sacred music and dance. Shortly after this Emanuel tries to use Western metaphysics and logic combined with physical force dictated by fear to deny the reality of what is happening to him. He demonstrates at the same time a mind and heart that is divided:

> What is this juju around my neck? Who's trying to cast spells on me? I don't believe in Macumba, I've already said so. (Long Pause.) But what if it's all true? What if this really is happening? After all . . . it is my people's religion. Just because I have a university degree, should I despise the worship in my blood? What if some Orixa is trying to keep me out of the whiteman's prison? (226)

This is a far cry from earlier statements and a testament to a conceptual shift in attitude toward himself. The dawning of his Afro-Brazilian consciousness is also the beginning of a mental retreat toward freedom from the yoke of slavery. The freedom is not material but psychological, emotional, social, and spiritual. A freedom capable only in spiritual ecstasy: "First, a feeling of peace, of fullness, then . . . sees that pregnant moon, rising so slowly? It is as if . . . as if I were riding it. . . . Nothing down here touches me anymore. Not even jail. . . . [A]ll the problems of this hard world, transformation is the exact word, I have been transformed" (227).

In this mode we find Emanuel's acceptance of his African ancestral faith, and subsequently he denounces Christianity as white witchcraft disguised as civilized faith. Then follows a quick turnaround where he once again challenges Exu. Paradoxically, in the process he unconsciously begins a ritual of worship of Òrìṣà. But Emanuel must travel deeper than these mere words of bravado and symbolic ritual performance of worship. He must de-westernize himself of all external paraphernalia of European codes of civility and spirituality. He must return to his roots naked, clothed only in the colors of his slain roots and cultural memory. Thus, we find him stripping himself of all the garments of upper-class respectability, what he now labels as "White benevolence: charity and compassion and civilized clown suit" (238). He disrobes himself physically and also metaphysically when he uses language to exorcise himself of white mis-education of Blacks: "Take this trash. With these lies and others you make black people lower their heads. You crush what pride they have. You lynch the poor bastards inside. And they're tamed, castrated, good little Negroes with white souls. Not me. No bit in my mouth. Imitating you like tamed monkeys. Until today I pretended" (238).

Again, we enter in a politicized religious chant of voices where racial war seems inevitable with the rise of Afrocentric consciousness generated from Afrocentric spirituality. But the call to action here to smash the white world's hypocrisy, annihilate false dreams of whiteness, defeat the white world's violence, obliterate the destructive power of the white world, and eradicate the white world's hate (239) is not a call to purge the world of white people. It is not a call for race annihilation or hatred. It is not a turning of the tables, but a ceremony of social purification that will cleanse Black people from the effects of white people's behavior. It is a call to exorcise from the psychological DNA of Blacks the corrosive effects of the illusion of whiteness as the ultimate reach. However, that cannot be done using the same techniques and tools of the white system. It can be attained through a conceptual and practical return to African spirituality. Emanuel, the representative Black male, must recognize that his name and his bloodline indicates that the god Exu Pelintru, Exu Tranca Ruas, Exu Barabo, the god of crossroads is with him at this crossroads of his life, to point out to him the path he must traverse toward freedom. The congregation of Filhas de Santos is there as a community of priestesses to aide him on through invocatory prayers to Exu to bless Emanuel and to give him safe passage, winning, wiliness, guile, understanding, courage, determination, lucidity, and love (239–40).

The prayer enables Emanuel to enter into the sacred shrine of Ogun to later emerge transfigured and translated. The journey into the *pegi* of Ogun is a corollary to a return to womb space where he must return to be born again. As he emerges from the *pegi* his language becomes prophetic and mystical. He is no longer the Emanuel from the beginning of the play, but a transfigured, resurrected one, one who now speaks with the voice of Babalorixa. He is the voice of the Yoruba/African gods: "In me Ogun's grave bloodflow spills over the dimensions of the first universe. Oh woeful division of the perfect being, the seamless magnificent body. Disintegrated, divided. I am the severed piece that floats in still steaming blood" (242). And later:

> Your voice is my ear, Ogun; my breath . . . my Saliva is your mouth that shouts me in the muteness of blood to blood. Parting . . . parting . . . we have been separated, we are divided. . . . Comparted in parts without parts. . . . Cosmorama whole and diverse which imparts and

dissevers us, yet primordial space calls for the return to continuance of being. Being arising . . . transcending . . . this human nature of mine . . . nature of ours derives from the hands of Obatala. This is my moment, my essence . . . my existence. My chaos, my abyss. I unclench my fist, and black birds are released to their dawning song. (242)

As Emanuel drinks of Ogun's wine and speaks of freedom, the rhythmic sounds of sacred drums intensify. The music of praise and solicitation calls to the various Yoruba gods, and, as the stage atmosphere becomes transformed into a ritual performance in which spiritual forces are also involved, Emanuel enters into his last moments of transfiguration and cries out in ecstatic joy: "In my breast, O, Oxumare, sparkles the reflection of your light, shining serpent who rainbows this midnight glow, generator of many marvels, that in my night I searched for and were given to me. In this absolute silence that I alone can hear, to the primal beings that my eyes alone can see, proclaim I celebrate" (243). The old Emanuel is sacrificed, giving way to a new beginning as the Iyalorixa pronounces: "Our *obligation* is almost performed. His about to begin. In *axé*'s dynamic continuum, in the mythical journey to the other face of existence. Emanuel is gone. He has become life's energy" (243).

This climactic movement is sanctified by the eruption of Shango's thunder and lightning, transforming the stage once more back into the historical time of the Palmares kingdom as Emanuel becomes the image of Zumbi. In dying he re-confirms the collective *ase* of the people. *Sortilege II: Zumbi Returns* provides a spiritualized drama in secular and artistic worlds; it takes us through the narrative performance of the humanization of the Yoruba deities in a diasporic environment. In so doing, the play deploys a strategic maneuver that creates an empathetic alliance between the gods and humans. Emanuel's sacrifice is a call for Afro-Brazilians to sacrifice the Eurocentric garments that stifle them, in order to realize who they really are and to use this liberation to erect new paradigms of individual and group survival. But sacrifice is not enough if it is not creative and if it does not lead to rebirth that is inclusive of all the peoples in the new world. This is where Gilkes's play points in the new direction. For instance, Gilkes's *Couvade*, though set principally in the home and art studio of the main character Lionel, is symbolically set in a forest clearing and opens with a shamanic ritual of invocation to the gods and spirits:

> On a totally darkened stage lights come up to reveal a small clearing in the Guyana rainforest. Filtering down the (invisible) upper storey of the trees—giant greenheart, mora, etc. the dappled moonlight picks out an Amerindian benab in which (there are no walls) a hammock is slung, its occupant asleep as in a cocoon or canoe of darkness. Background noises: sound of tree frog, cicada, the occasional cry of a goatsucker ("who you?") fade in and hold for about 20 seconds. Music comes up as background noises gradually fade. Very faintly but growing louder as it approaches, the music is a weird mixture of gourd, flute, deep braying bamboo, horn, drum; the discordant but clear bone flute melody rising above a gentle slow, but definite rhythm . . . attractive, ethereal. (1)

This magical and sacred setting enables the priestly figures to perform rituals that open up the portals through which the gods and ancestral spirits anthropomorphically pass through into the human world to help reveal the paths to redemption to those attuned to their presence. The shaman figure is described as "an incredibly old man . . . frail as ash; his skin pouched and wrinkled, papery-thin like a spider's or a lizard's. His voice is . . . tired and authoritative, suggesting power as well as suffering" (1). The ethereal figure enters into the dreamscape and real world of the figure asleep in the hammock and speaks to the sleeper through his dreams. This entry into the subconscious of the sleeper awakens the dormant memory cells to help ignite and initiate action. This dramaturgical strophe reveals the dormant historical memories of Guyanese of every ethnic background and demonstrates the symbiotic relationship among these groups in the formation of the national Guyanese personhood. By entering into and stirring the repressed unconscious of Guyanese people, the shaman and his invocatory use of sacred ritual chant release the buried desires of Guyanese people for cultural, spiritual, artistic, racial, and sociopolitical liberation from the traumatic histories that seem to tie them down to despair.

The gentle and imperceptible entry of the shaman into the unconscious world of the dreamer is achieved through the medium of storytelling stringed with prayer. The constructed sacred yet secularized space for the performance of the various myths links *Couvade* to *Sortilege II: Zumbi Returns* and *Shango de Irma*. The playwrights deploy performative myth in ritual dramas in which invocatory prayers, music, and narratives become tools to open up the sealed portals of ancestral African, Asian, and

Amerindian ancestors. The invocation begins with an offertory prayer: "Hear, O Makanater / Your children ask you / To receive these offering / (manioc, milk of the calabash, land, and words of the heart)" (2). The prayer solicits the great Amerindian Makanater to guide the path of the lost pilgrims. This is justified through the muted lamentation revealed in the shaman's address to the sleeper/dreamer; that is, present-day Guyanese need to beware of the disappearance of their histories, cultures, land, language, and spiritualties as they continue to clutch the sleep caused by imperialism and racist cultural narratives:

> Sleep Couvade
> Dream your dream
> When you wake
> Forest will die
> Deer Tiger Tapir howler-monkey
> Die.
> Fishes will die
> Tukú'u, Guacháro will fly away
> Behind the cloud
> Our people die
> Cause of Makanater
> Will not sail across the sky
> Sleep Couvade
> Dream your dream. (2–3)

The shamanic lament originates in a prophetic vision that sees the death of the desire to live, to regenerate and reconnect with the ancestral ways in order to understand which path to take to save the future represented by the yet-to-be-born child of the dreamer, Lionel, and his wife, Pat. That path to recovery must be sought through art seething through the faces peering through Lionel's paintings. However, for Pat, the faces on Lionel's canvas are just faces. She cannot see beyond the material value of art and hence becomes a partial spokesvoice for those in Guyana who are almost lost in the dense linguistic and cultural forests of Eurocentric worldviews. To Lionel, on the other hand, the shamanic pronouncements become translated into representational art of remembering and reconnecting with pasts that make up the cosmic world of Guyanese.

Pat: What are all those faces supposed to be?
Lionel: Ancestral icons.
Pat: Ancestral who?

> Lionel: Icons. You know, like the carved figures on aboriginal totems.
> These . . . these are Guyanese icons. Ancestral images
> that go back to pre-Columbian past. . . .
> Pat: Look at this. Couvade. You and your Amerindian myths.
> Who would want to spend money on that? (6–7)

Pat's blindness to the sacred, mystical, and mythical value of Lionel's art and the role art plays in the process of re-membering and re-constructing one's past as a way of moving forward is caused by a cash-nexus value system inherited from her neocolonial education. She cannot see beyond the Western capitalist commoditization of art and begin to comprehend the sacred and symbolic in Lionel's art.

Pat's myopic understanding here is symptomatically and symbolically limited by the commercial view of art and originates in the negative self-recognition manifested in her espousal of internalized autoracism. She lambasts Lionel and his friends for their dreams of a cultural and racial awakening. Nonetheless, she is an unconscious participant in the move to a future that ensures a cultural and spiritual regeneration: through her womb. She is carrying Lionel's child, who is the ultimate synthesis or symbiotic fusion of all Guyana's cultures, traditions, and ethnicities. Hence, the shaman's ritualized opening prayer becomes much more urgent as it structures a counterdiscourse to Pat's consumerist's position. It sharpens Lionel's sensibilities and opens up his creative portals to revelatory visions. These visions must be translated onto canvas as portals to egalitarian race-remembrance and cultural recreation of the lost worlds of Amerindians, Africans, and Asians.

> Lionel: Pat. What do you think our son will look like, eh?
> A Douglah mother and an even more mixed-up father. . . .
> Did I even tell you that my grandfather was a push-knocker?
> Part African and part Amerindian? He did appeared somewhere
> up the Demerara River . . .
> Pat: Yes. Yes. And your grandmother was a Portuguese from Madeira
> and your maternal grandfather was an Indian from India. . . . (9)

In scene 4 of the play (14–15), we are presented with a hallowed West African ancestral presence signaled by sacred music, sounds, and a traditional religious priest. Interestingly, his invocatory prayers are verbatim repetitions of Akan and other African invocatory (14–15), ritual, and ceremonial drum language. This scene raises a legitimate issue of whether Gilkes at this point falls into the allure of what Soyinka sees as the zeal of a cultural promoter rather than "that of a truly communicant medium in what is essentially a 'rite of passage'" (5). Nonetheless, this section of the play reveals the mental confusions of the characters as the lust for material prosperity, an elusive ideal, complicates their community and reveals fissures in their psychological makeups. What is pertinent, however, at the play's core is the constant shift back to the ideal of cultural retrieval. This is set in contradistinction to the schizophrenic set, which is at once comic, irreverent, and irrelevantly out of place, where a group of half-baked Christians preaches the gospel of redemption through being born again according to Jesus. The message is convoluted, exclusionary, and terroristic in both language and delivery, and this undermines any project of a humane, orderly redemption Christianity may offer, save through punitive measures (42–46).

In contrast to the Christian group, scene 10 does not show a Lionel possessed by exclusionary Indian, African, Amerindian ancestors, so he is able to embark on his project to create a painting that is inclusive of all and that subsequently will have the power to enlighten others. Lionel is "painting feverishly—adding touches to a fantastic canvas: the figure of a composite man, something like an Aztec/Toltec totem, made up of African/Amerindian/Hindu elements, a half-human, half-animal/bird thing" (46). The questions here are several: How does one capture the spirit force, the essence, the Nommo in art? How can art truly reflect the dream and the message? How can art open the portal "between dream and reality? Living and dead: between past and present; And I have to open the door and walk through it!" (48).

Again, Lionel's nightmarish cry of pain transfers the scene back to the forest where magic is once more at work. The nightmare is a vehicle through which he enters into the world of the visionary where his eyes behold a convergence of all the ancestral spirits and images from various continents. In this trance state, Lionel becomes the canvas of communication through whom the painting becomes not just the medium, but also the message. He is anointed and transformed into the messenger who must get the message of the ancestors across to the people (50–51). He paints his face with the colors of white, black, and red and is draped in a gown of protection. Thus, he is now priest, prophet, and warrior. He is triply empowered by the African and Amerindian ancestors (31–32). He is the mask of ancestors: "Shaman. See! Couvade sleeps. Son of Manater sleeps. *We* are his dreams. All the old ones, all the young ones, all the women, all the men, all the little ones, all the great ones. Everything that lives; plants, trees. Dust of manioc, milk of the earth. He dreams us all" (32). In this dream, he is given the garment of responsibility and service to his community even if it means self-sacrifice: "Receive, Couvade, this robe of the sun. Great Earthmaker look kindly on our people" (51). Meanwhile, during all this time, there is ritual dancing and music reflecting a combination of Chinese, Indian, Amerindian, West African, and European sources. The stage directions give us an idea of this symbiosis of peoples that make up the Caribbean culturescape: "a human totem made up of three dancers; the lowest (squatting) in Arawak, the middle (half stooping) in West African, and the topmost in Southern Indian ritual costume. The 'totem' moves its arms in a gentle, undulating rhythm—a suggestion of Shiva, the creator/destroyer—there is a new sound, a rhythm, bell-like sound, as Carib dancers . . ." (49–51).

Gilkes's description here reinforces a hierarchical, racist, three-tier system of cultural mixing in which the Caribs form the base foundation, Africans the mid-section, and South Asians the top. There is very little creativity here except the re-inscription of a Eurocentric racist and hierarchical reading of society in Guyana. Yet when Lionel is ordained and authorized to be the conduit of ancestral recuperation, only the Amerindian shaman and the African priest are celebrated. In his waking hours, he tries to convince his friend Arthur, the Afrocentric eccentric whose cultural myopia and racialized politics of exclusion make him reject the reality of racial and cultural mixing in Guyana and argue that "you and your tolerance! All this talk about the 'seeds of different cultures.' That is just a load of bullshit! Like your Amerindian myths" (25–26). However, in the hospital Arthur seems to be beginning to comprehend Lionel's vision as something beyond the reach of politics when he is finally ready to listen to Lionel's dream of not working for himself but for the future generations: "I must learn the dances. Not for myself, you see. For the others. I have to teach them the dances. Teach them what I learn. Do you understand? All things are part of one wholeness. One mandala" (60). The play suddenly ends with a ritual offering of a prayer of thanksgiving and supplication by priest and shaman.

The words of Lionel are a fitting place to bring this chapter to a close. If we look at the three plays as a ritual and mythopoeic cycle involving African Caribbean and Afro-Brazilian drama of African recuperation and re-connection, it is evident they echo a certain spiritual and mythic unity of radical purpose though not through any prior plan by the authors. My initial hunch to begin my discussion with *Shango de Irma* seems to have been fortuitous because I now see how *Shango de Irma* establishes the directions that these playwrights suggest (though not prescribe) that African Caribbean and Afro-Brazilian people must follow to create the right psycho-spiritual and cultural environments for meaningful and lasting recuperative collective and individual selfhoods. Here they reject both Walcott's and Césaire's pessimism that the African deities are dead or deaf and have forgotten their children in Diaspora.

These plays become the *abengs* with which they call for awakening. In that awakening, Emanuel's murder of his white wife is a symbolic act of violent exorcism. It echoes Walcott's trial scene in *Dream on Monkey Mountain* and the execution of white characters involved in the transatlantic slave trade. Also there is a connection with Makak and Lestrade's act of exorcism of African Caribbean male/female desires to equal the whites by way of sexual relations with the white women/men (Fanon 41–82). Thus, because European cultural indoctrination of the African Caribbean and Afro-Brazilian was done through violence, only the violence associated with exorcism can get rid of this desire for whiteness. For the male heroes in these plays, the illusion of whiteness must be violently excised through the symbolic act of ritual killing of whiteness represented by white women in their lives. It is only through this ritual of sacrifice that Emanuel finally attains psychological, cultural, and emotional peace and empowerment. But he could not have done this alone without the spiritual rituals performed by the Iyalorixa. Thus, Emanuel's transfiguration and transformation in *Sortelige II: Zumbi Returns* is indirectly linked to Lionel's conviction that the portal of entry into the world of racial and cultural harmony in his spirit is opened through a garment of cultural, religious, racial, historical, linguistic, and artistic inclusivity. Thus, unlike *Sortilege II: Zumbi Returns*, which ends in death and the total rejection of other cultural and spiritual realities that had imprisoned Emanuel, *Couvade* ends with the promise of a birth of a new African Diasporic person that reflects all cultural, spiritual, and racial possibilities in the Caribbean.

In his attempt to achieve this harmony of multiple realities and dreams, Gilkes sacrifices the potentialities of the mythic sections of the play. The play at these heightened moments of expectations then runs out of steam and languishes in an assemblage of sociopolitical clichés, regurgitated ethnographic recordings, and even replications of racist readings of Guyanese cultures. Nonetheless, the play's engagement of drums and music secures what Harrison describes as "communal participation in both sacred and secular ceremonies" within the African world ("Mother/ Word" xxxiv). Following on the lead of Abraham's observation at an Akan ceremonial performance, Harrison writes that "the need to adapt musical aids to the proceedings without submerging the verbal account forced the raconteur to seek musical qualities in . . . words" (91). Hence, Gilkes's engagement of what might be termed authentic African and Amerindian language, music, dance, incantations, prayers, supplications, and blessings at various climaxes of the play gives the play a performative verisimilitude. He captures what Nathaniel McKay defines as the "phantom limb [that] arises from [its] capacity for feeling. . . . Phantom . . . is a relativizing term which cuts both ways, occasioning a shift in perspective between real and spiritual, an exchange of attributes between the two" (34). The use of music to initialize the action also becomes a destabilizing maneuver of time and space in order to create and maintain the magical setting needed to begin the ritual myth performance/narrative. Without the creation of the sacred setting, the gods cannot be invoked to stage their own story for the education and edification of humans. Thus, the success of *Couvade*, unlike the other plays, does not rest in its political message alone but in its initiatory attempt to realize in art form the complicated quilt of Cuban and Brazilian societies in particular and all societies in the Americas in general based on the realities of cultural, social, racial, and linguistic pluralities. The plays demonstrate the difficulty faced by artists, dramatists, poets, and politicians to formulate and articulate a unified vision of the new African in the Americas from the shifting identities.

NOTE

A portion of this chapter was previously published with the same title in "Of Rebels, Tricksters, and Supernatural Beings: Toward a Semiotics of Myth Performance in African Diaspora Drama." *Anansi's Defiant Webs: Contact, Continuity, Convergence, and Complexity in the Languages, Literatures, and Cultures of the Greater Caribbean*. Eds. Faraclas, Nicholas, Ronald Severing, Christa Weijer, Liesbeth Echteld, and Marsha Hinds-Layne. Curaçao/Puerto Rico: Fundashon pa Planifikashon Idioma (Institute for Language Planning of Curaçao) and Universidad di Kòrsou (University of the Curaçao). 199–211. Print.

WORKS CITED

Abraham, W. E. *The Mind of Africa*. Chicago: U of Chicago P. 1962. Print.

Boas, Fraser. *The World of Myth: Talking with Joseph Campbell*. Boston: Shambhala. 1994. Print.

Campbell, Joseph. *The Way of Myth: Talking with Fraser Boas*. Boston: Shambahala. 1994. Print.

Carril, Pepe. *Shango de Irma: A Yoruba Mystery Play*. English adaptation with a preface by Susan Sherman. Introduction by Jerome Rethenberg and Edward James. Garden City, NY: Doubleday and Company, 1969, 1970. Print.

Césaire, Aimé. *And the Dogs Were Silent. Lyric and Dramatic Poetry 1946–82*. Trans. Clayton Eshleman and Annette Smith. Charlottesville: UP of Virginia, 1996, 1999. 3–74. Print.

de Graft, Joe. "Roots in African Drama and Theatre." *Black Theatre: Ritual Performance in the African Diaspora*. Ed. Paul Carter Harrison, Victor Leo Walker Jr., and Gus Edwards. Philadelphia: Temple UP, 2002. 18–38. Print.

Drewal, Henry John. *African Artistry: Techniques and Aesthetics in Yorùbá Sculpture*. Atlanta: High Museum of Art, 1980. Print.

Drewal, Henry John, and John Pemberton III with Rowland Abiodun. *Yorùbá: Nine Centuries of African Art and Thought*. New York: Center of African Art in association with Harry N. Abraham, 1989. Print.

Drewal, Margaret T. *Yorùbá Ritual; Performance, Play, Agency*. Bloomington: Indiana UP, 1992. Print.

Edmunds, Laura. "The Literary Manifestation of Xangô in Brazil: Esmeralda Ribeiro's 'A procura de uma borboleta preta.'" *ṢÁNGÒ in Africa and African Diaspora*. Ed. Joel E. Tishken, Tóyìn Fálọlá, and Akíntúrndé Akínyẹmí. Bloomington: Indiana UP, 2009. 273–83. Print.

Fanon, Frantz. *Black Skin, White Masks*. Trans. from original French by Charles Lam Markmann. New York: Grove, 1967. Print.

Gilbert, Helen, and Joanne Tompkins. *Post-colonial Drama: Theory, Practice, Politics*. London: Routledge, 1976. Print.

Gilkes, Michael. *Couvade: A Dream-Play of Guyana*. London: Dongaroo, 1988. Print.

Glazier, Stephen D. "Withre Ṣàngó? An Inquiry into Ṣàngó's Authenticity and Prominence in the Caribbean." *ṢÁNGÒ in Africa and African Diaspora*. Ed. Joel E. Tishken, Tóyìn Fálọlá, and Akíntúrndé Akínyẹmí. Bloomington: Indiana UP, 2009. Print.

Glissant, Edouard. *Caribbean Discourse: Selected Essays*. Trans. Michael Dash. Charlottesville: UP of Virginia, 1999. Print.

Götrick, Kacke. *Apidan Theatre and Modern Drama: A Study in a Traditional Yoruba Theatre and Its Influence on Modern Drama by Yoruba Playwrights*. Stockholm, Sweden: Almqvist and Wiksell International, 1984. Print.

Harrison, Paul Carter. "Mother/Word." *Totem Voices: Plays from the Black World Repertory*. New York: Grove, 1989. Print.

———. "Praise/Word." *Black Theatre: Ritual Performance in the African Diaspora*. Ed. Paul Carter Harrison, Victor Leo Walker Jr., and Gus Edwards. Philadelphia: Temple UP, 2002. 1–10. Print.

Hatch, James V., and Errol G. Hill. *A History of African American Theatre*. Cambridge Studies in American Theatre and Drama. Cambridge: Cambridge UP, 2003. Print.

Herskovitz, M. J., and F. J. Herskovitz, eds. *Dahomean Narrative: A Cross-Cultural Analysis*. Evanston: Northwestern UP, 1968. 3–122. Print.

Irobi, Esiala. "In the Theory of Ase: The Persistence of African Performance Aesthetics in the North American Diaspora—August Wilson, Ntozake Shange and Djanet Sears." *African Theatre 8: Diasporas*. Ed. James Gibbs et al. Bristol: James Currey, 2009. Print.

Kuwabong, Dannabang. "Of Rebels, Tricksters, and Supernatural Beings: Toward a Semiotics of Myth Performance in African Diaspora Drama." *Anansi's Defiant Webs: Contact, Continuity, Convergence, and Complexity in the Languages, Literatures, and Cultures of the Greater Caribbean*. Ed. Nicholas Faraclas, Ronald Severing, Christa Weijer, Liesbeth Echteld, and Marsha Hinds-Layne. Curaçao/Puerto Rico: Fundashon pa Planifikashon di Idioma

(Institute for Language Planning of Curaçao) and Universidad di Kòrsou (University of the Curaçao), 2011. 199–211. Print.

———. "Performances that Bind: A Preliminary Reading of Dramaturgic Elements in Ngugi wa ThiongÓ's *I Will Marry When I Want*, Derek Walcott's *Dream on Monkey Mountain*, August Wilson's *The Piano Lesson* and Aime Cesaire's *And the Dogs Were Silent.*" *Re-Centering the "Islands in Between": Rethinking the Languages, Literatures, and Cultures of the Eastern Caribbean and the Diaspora.* Ed. N. Faraclas, R. Severing, C. Weijer, and E. Echteld. Willemstad, Curaçao: Fundashon pa Planifikashon di Idioma, 2009. Print.

Lawal, Babatunde. "The African Heritage in African American Art and Performance." *Black Theatre: Ritual Performance in the African Diaspora.* Ed. Paul Carter Harrison, Victor Leo Walker Jr., and Gus Edwards. Philadelphia: Temple UP, 2002. 39–63. Print.

———. "From Africa to the Americas." *Santeria Aesthetics in Contemporary Latin American Art.* Ed. Arturo Lindsay. Washington, DC: Smithsonian Institution Press, 1996. Print.

Locke, Alain, and Montgomery Gregory, eds. *Plays of Negro Life: A Source Book of Negro American Drama.* Decorations and Illustrations by Douglas Aaron. New York: Harper and Brothers, 1927. Print.

McKay, Nathaniel. "Sound and Sentiment, Sound and Symbol." *Callaloo* 30.1 (1987): 28–54. Print.

Murphy, Joseph M. *Santeria: An African Religion in America.* Boston: Beacon Press, 1988. Print.

Nascimento, Abdias do. Introduction. *Sortilege (Black Mystery).* Trans. Peter Lownds. Chicago: Third World Press, 1978. Iii. Print.

——— *Sortilege II: Zumbi Returns.* Trans. with introduction by Elisa Larkin Nascimento. *Crosswinds: An Anthology of Black Dramatists in the Diaspora.* Ed. with introduction by William B. Branch. Bloomington: Indiana UP, 1993. 203–49. Print.

Nascimento, Elisa Larkin. Introduction to *Sortilege II: Zumbi Returns. Crosswinds: An Anthology of Black Dramatists in the Diaspora.* Ed. with introduction by William B. Branch. Bloomington: Indiana UP, 1993. 203–6. Print.

Parés, Luis Nicolan. "Xangô in Afro-Brazilian Religion: 'Aristocracy' and 'Syncretic' Interactions." *ṢÀNGÒ in Africa and African Diaspora.* Ed. Joel E. Tishken, Tóyìn Fálọlá, and Akíntúndé Akínyẹmí. Bloomington: Indiana UP, 2009. 248–72. Print.

Santiago, Miguel F. *Dancing with the Saints: An Exploration of Santeria's Sacred Tools: Initiation, Possession, Animal Sacrifice, Divination, Music, Chant and Dance as Vehicles of Integration and Transformation.* Puerto Rico: Inter American University, 1993. Print.

Skidmore, Thomas E. *Black into White: Race and Nationality in Brazilian Thought.* New York: Oxford UP, 1974. Print.

Soyinka, Wole. *Myth, Literature, and the African World.* Cambridge: Cambridge UP, 1976. Print.

Stoval, Tyler. "Black Community Black Spectacles: Performance and Race in Transatlantic Perspective." *Black Cultural Traffic: Crossroads in Global Performance and Popular Culture.* Ed. Harry J. Elam Jr. and Kennell Jackson. Ann Arbor: U of Michigan P, 2008. 221–41. Print.

Thompson, Robert Farris. *Flash of the Spirit: African and Afro-American Art and Philosophy.* New York: Vintage, 1984. Print.

Walcott, Derek. "What the Twilight Says: An Overture." *Dream on Monkey Mountain and Other Plays.* New York: Farrar, Straus and Giroux, 1970. 3–40. Print.

Walker, Victor Leo, Jr. Introduction to *Black Theatre: Ritual Performance in the African Diaspora.* Ed. Paul Carter Harrison, Victor Leo Walker Jr., and Gus Edwards. Philadelphia: Temple UP, 2002. 13–17. Print.

White, Hayden. *Metahistory: The Historical Imagination in Nineteenth Century Europe.* Baltimore: The Johns Hopkins UP, 1973. Print.

Wright, Jay. "Desire's Design, Vision's Resonance: Black Poetry's Ritual and Historical Voice." *Callaloo,* no. 30 (Winter, 1987): 13–28. Print.

6

OF PRINCESSES AND QUEENS

The Mythical Journeys Home in Djanet Sears's *Afrika,*
Solo and Rebecca Fisseha's *Wise.Woman*

Christopher Olsen

Disaporic studies have expanded considerably in the last twenty years, ever since the initial focus centered on minority cultures experiencing forced exile from their homeland. The term "diaspora," as Shaleen Singh (2008) points out, has undergone a conversion and now encompasses a much wider definition. During the 1990s, William Safran and Robin Cohen wrote seminal articles attempting to designate the common features of a diaspora via a list of examples that included such goals as a desire for reverse migration and a belief in finding an ancestral home. Safran's and Cohen's lists were not the same, but they shared a number of characteristics. Safran, who focuses on an original definition of diasporic peoples as seen through the events of the Jewish Holocaust, provides a list that includes the following: "Retain a collective memory or myth of their homeland," and "Committed to the maintenance and restoration of their original homeland" (90). Cohen's list includes the following: "A collective memory and myth about the homeland, including its locating history and achievements," and "An idealization of the putative ancestral home and a collective commitment to its maintenance, restoration, safety, and prosperity, even to its creation" (515). Cohen goes on to mention that the identification with a diaspora serves to bridge the gap between the local and the global (516).

Both authors point to problems in identifying these connections, but Safran questions how much time is required to develop this consciousness: "How long does it take for a diaspora consciousness to develop, and what are the necessary and sufficient conditions for its survival?" (95). What is implied in developing this diasporic consciousness is a belief that one must make return to the homeland via an actual physical journey or through vicarious contact with your ancestral peoples. With regard to Africa, many scholars have pointed out that the problems with engaging with one's past can be shaped by a Black Diasporic discourse. Zara Bennett provides an example from Eddy L. Harris's account of visiting the slave museum at Goreé Island and his concern not only of how he will be received in Africa but how he will respond to his mythical expectations of what modern Africa is. The fear is that too much history has separated them (13). Sandra L. Richards writes about visiting the Elmina and Cape Coast castles, which have been turned into museums on slave history. She points to the perceptions of African American visitors who find they want an emotional stake in this "tourist" attraction that is commemorating human suffering on an immense scale (618). As she points out, African North Americans need to locate their identities even in the face of repression—or, as Bennett suggests, diasporic travelers interpret their ancestral home through a "filter."

There are problems in making a journey back to one's homeland—a reverse migration, if you will—because, as Robin Cohen points out when describing homeland and cultural diasporas, these "travelers" must balance their nostalgic desire to return to their homeland to join the majority with their present condition as members of a minority. Their journey can turn into a circular run whereby travelers keep returning to the same place they started. These "black diasporic pilgrims," as Bennett calls them, often insert themselves into an African setting, focusing on their metaphysical and spiritual changes but sometimes losing a sense of the African context (8). They never quite allow themselves to totally become one identity or the other.

One usually associates comedians, performance artists, and storytellers with the revealing of multiple identities. Often you can find stand-up comedians telling stories from their youth such as Bill Cosby did with his Fat Albert stories. You can see this form in certain performance art pieces by women as in the work of Chicano female playwrights Cherrie Moraga and Monica Palacios. Sometimes, in an ensemble piece performers come to represent symbols (and, by extension, identities) within a culture such as Ntozake Shange's *For Colored Girls Who Have Considered Suicide When the Rainbow Is Enuf.* The purpose of this technique is to cross the boundaries of linear storytelling by experimenting with different visual and vocal sensations, embodying multiple characters, and crossing over into other historical periods. Joanne Tompkins quotes from Wilson Harris's Caribbean novel *The Infinite Rehearsal* and uses the title to describe diasporic performances on stage, in particular, when performers engage in repetitive sequences that may seem to be endless as they keep searching and discarding various attempts at connecting to their homeland via their ancestral journey (35).

Djanet Sears is a Canadian playwright who has been writing about race, gender issues, and collective identity for twenty-five years. All of her main characters are women who confront a white-dominated culture and who grapple with not only the injustices of present Canadian society but also those from the past. Sears draws from her childhood experiences growing up in Canada and identifies herself as African Canadian. *Afrika, Solo* (1987) was her first major play. Rebecca Fisseha is a young Canadian playwright from Toronto who has written several plays about her experience with her Ethiopian homeland.

Both Sears's *Afrika, Solo* and Fisseha's *Wise.Woman* are about a journey of discovery and of reverse migration. Sears's Djanet is a Western woman who returns to her geographic and ancestral roots to challenge her mythical (and sometimes misguided) idea of what it means to be African. Fisseha's Saba, also a Western woman, journeys back to Ethiopia to join her fiancé and assume a new identity as a wife of an Ethiopian man. Although both characters are Canadian citizens, Djanet was born half Jamaican, half Guyanese, and Saba is of Ethiopian descent. Both women make discoveries at the end of their journeys that cause them to reconsider their initial plans and to experience what Zara Bennett called "The Foiled Myth of Return." Although their journeys home may have been disappointing, they are also enlightening because the traveling "pilgrims" have made further discoveries about their mythical homeland and use this newfound knowledge as an anchor to help them navigate the choppy cultural waters that make up modern Africa.

Sears's play is comprised of a series of montages in which scenes are interrupted by sudden changes of venue or quick bursts of music. For example, the opening scene of *Afrika, Solo* features a young woman

(Sears's alter ego) who is saying good-bye to her African lover, Ben, in his bedroom. He is not present, but she has just packed up her things and left a farewell note on his bed. Suddenly, the quiet moment is interrupted by loud music, and she turns herself into a rap singer accompanied by two male musicians who function as a kind of chorus throughout the play. She sings the following:

> It took a trip to Africa to find my root,
> Let me tell ya, what I saw did not compute.
> Not everyone was starving like they tell you on TV,
> I never met an African who lived on a tree.
> They're much more concerned with warthogs and vultures,
> Than for African people, their history and cultures.
> The Kingdom of Mali was rich and strong.
> It was four months wide and four months long.
> Have you ever heard of Hausa land,
> Ancient Ghana, and, and, and . . .
> Songhai, Bornu, Abomey, look,
> We need to rewrite the history book. [1]
> I'm gonna tell 'bout the journey and what happened to me,
> So relax and listen and you will see.
> Toronto to Tombouctou,
> Nairobi to Ouagadougou.
> Fasten your belt, takeoff's begun,
> Seven, six, five, four, three, two . . . (6)

This modern woman emerges out of one corner of the African Diaspora (in Canada) and chooses to embark on an odyssey to reconnect and learn about her ancestors. It is a physical as well as a metaphysical journey that echoes what Djanet tells us about her childhood when she was fascinated with science fiction television programs. She has literally taken a plane to visit Africa, but her reference to a seatbelt acts as a metaphor that suggests that she needs some additional protection in case the cultural divide between Africa and Canada gets choppy. During Sears's childhood, she may have taken off and journeyed to other galaxies, but she lands in the "alien" confines of the airport at Contonou, Benin, where she is trying to get a ticket to leave Africa and return to Canada.

Fisseha's Saba also starts her journey at the airport—but the one at Addis Ababa, Ethiopia, where she is trying to contact her fiancé, Solomon. Fisseha's odyssey also begins in modern-day Africa (Ethiopia), but her connection involves oscillating between two worlds—the ancient world of the queen of Sheba and the modern life of a director for Ethiopian tours. Saba and her ancient muse, Sheba, are both headed to meet men who would like to become their husbands and who are both named Solomon. Sears has chosen to change her name to Djanet (from Janet), which she says means "paradise" in Arabic and is an oasis town in the Sahara Desert. Djanet has also found a potential partner in Ben, a French-born citizen of Benin. Both Djanet and Saba, as well as Sheba, return to their homes sadder but wiser. The mythical Sheba speaks for both modern women, saying, "I turn not toward my mother's land, but into my own" (60).

It can be argued that *Afrika, Solo* belongs to a feminist genre because the main character engages in the viability of her multiple identities that have been forced upon her by a patriarchal world. *Wise.Woman* can also be construed as having a feminist leaning, primarily because the main character identifies strongly with the mythical queen of Sheba, a woman who defied ancient patriarchal expectations. Fisseha's play is more linear with the main character existing in two dimensions—in the ancient world and in the modern. By the end of the play, Fisseha's Saba is facing her future having learned about her own multiple identities through her interaction with an ancient figure; except that these identities have fused into one identity—a strong woman whose past and present are clearly intertwined. Sears's play is more circular: Djanet is trying to make sense of the African/Canadian divide, and she too learns about her multiple identities as she returns to face her adopted homeland. Marlene Moser has stated that *Afrika, Solo* can be seen through a "feminist standpoint position" where Djanet manages to combine the subject with the object, the global with the personal (241–42). Moser cites Tompkins's term "autobio-mythography" to describe a writer who uses her/his onstage body as "archives of cultural and individual memory" and who creates a connection between the subjects onstage and off. She points to what Jill Dolan called "utopian performatives," which are performances that produce communal moments between actors and audience (455).

Each playwright uses a different methodology to reveal the journey of her female protagonist. Sears uses an almost confessional approach, embodying and mimicking many characters of her childhood, much like a storyteller or comedian would do. She begins telling her audience about a confusing upbringing in Canada and launches into her early childhood memories of a thinly veiled racist world filled with false icons. She

Figure 6.1. Djanet Sears in *Afrika, Solo.* Photo by Peter Freund, courtesy of the photographer.

evokes celluloid images and musical themes from television shows and films that drew her attention as a child growing up in a white Western world. She imagines herself as somewhat of a cultural explorer in the paternalistic mode of the 1960s American space saga *Star Trek,* whose motto is "to go where no *man* has gone before" and whose "prime directive" is to locate new galaxies and integrate with the aliens peacefully and never to colonize them. Her fantasy, however, soon dissolves as she begins to question the logic and appearance of other supposed benevolent space pioneers—such as the British TV figure Doctor Who—and then wonders why characters in space sagas seem so young and attractive. Feeling insecure about her dark-skinned appearance and her full body, the adolescent Janet finds solace in imagining herself resembling Dorothy Dandridge, a Black actress whom Hollywood turned into a kind of exotic native woman and who became acceptable as a sexual fantasy figure for white audiences. The fantasy begins to unravel when Sears recounts the Hollywood manipulation of the Tarzan movies (she loves to yell out the Tarzan primal cry) as a defense of colonialism—complete with Tarzan's bad American accent and his "native" sidekick, Cheeta the Chimpanzee, who apparently was so attracted to his master that during filming he had a constant erection which required makeup artists to paint it black. Nevertheless, armed with her misshapen childhood fantasies, she embarks on this ancestral journey and finds herself recalling some of the sensations and images of Africa, such as the chanting, drumming, and storytelling among different tribal groups.

Fisseha begins with a historical reenactment of a myth when the queen of Sheba decides to make a trip across the desert to the city of Axum in a caravan. She wants to meet the powerful King Solomon, who is noted for his wisdom and sexual proclivity. She is joined by her trusted aid, Tamrin, who functions as the conscience of the society around her, a kind of chorus leader, who introduces her to the powerful King Solomon by several names including Mak'da, Azeb, Bilquis, and—ultimately—Saba. Saba, the modern descendant of Sheba, opens the play upon her arrival at the Addis Ababa airport to marry an Ethiopian man whom she met as an adolescent. According to Tamrin, Saba means "she who follows her footprints, crossing distances believing there to be sweetness and joy deeper than her own" (4). Fisseha creates two parallel scenarios with actors playing parts in both segments. Sheba/Saba function as protagonists who meet King Solomon/Fiancé Solomon while the other characters function as kind of a chorus. Tamrin, for example, turns into a pushy store owner in the airport, insisting that Saba buy an antique Ethiopian shawl. As the play progresses, Saba's attempts to integrate into modern Ethiopia become intertwined with the ancient myth of Sheba and Solomon. It is as if Saba is being guided by the myth of Sheba.

In contrast to Saba, Djanet relives a disturbing moment of truth during her childhood that would later inspire her to set off on this ancestral journey. In recounting her childhood fantasies, she playfully tries to make sense of one idea and gives up before launching into another. She starts talking about how people on television are so beautiful, and then she wonders about her own hair and what color wigs she should use. It is very childlike and reveals an uncertainty about the relationship between celluloid identities and real ones. But it is her flighty white friend, VD, who unwittingly reminds her of her "true identity" in the Canadian ethnographic landscape. Djanet, VD, and a boy named Keith are sitting in a cafeteria at school and are deciding who should be made to eat the hated cauliflower that is being served to them. VD decides to use the familiar nursery rhyme, "Eenie, meenie, miny, mo" to determine who would have to eat it, except she uses the old racist version of the second line: "catch a nigger by the toe." Djanet gets very upset and slaps her friend, which causes VD to summon her much bigger brother, Terminal, who hits Djanet in the face, breaking two of her teeth. After this horrible incident, the two former friends meet once more, and unrepentantly VD tells Djanet, "Why don't you just go back where you came from!" (15). This confuses the child, but the grown woman waiting at the airport to return to her country wonders what that statement really means.

> Mother is from Jamaica, But my dad, he's from Guyana . . .
> And I was born in England, the same as V.D.
>
> God save our gracious queen
> Long live our noble queen
> God save our queen . . .
>
> If I was born in Gdansk, am I a pole?
> I may be *Solidarnoc*; but I've got soul.
> I talk like a Brit from Saskatoon,
> And let me tell ya, it's no damn honeymoon.
> I call one day about a room for rent.
> When I get to the house, he says "It just went."

And it happens all the time and it makes me wanna foam.
I just gotta get away, I'm gonna find my home.
There's no place like home. There's no place like home.
There's no place like home. (16)

Djanet decides to adopt a new identity of a long-lost African princess
who is returning to her ancestral home after spending her whole life in
another world. She arrives in Tunisia and catches her first sight of the
Sahara Desert. Upon seeing the desert for the first time, she exclaims,
"Living in the Sahara is like living on another planet. Yeah, I felt as if I
were on Mars" (19). But as she becomes more accustomed to the terrain
she exclaims, "I'd never be able to wash the African sand from out of my
soul" (20). She finally arrives at the oasis town of Djanet, which provides
her with a new name, and she continues on to see ancient rock paintings
near the Tassli plateau. It is here that she marvels at the age of her
ancestors and how long they have been on this earth. Again, she reminds
the audience that African myth has been created by Western anthropologists. "Have you noticed that if an anthropologist goes out and studies an
ancient 'third world' culture, and he finds knowledge of traditions way in
advance of his own, he always ends up speculating on visitations from
outer space" (21). At another moment she wonders cynically: "You
know, nothing exists until a white man finds it!" (23).

Djanet's quest to find a mythical Africa that she can identify with
never fully materializes, although there are moments when she finds a
home she feels an affinity for. She begins with a "short-lived excursion
into Christianity" in Kenya where she lives among the Turkana people
and is amazed to find that her Turkana host, David, is Muslim and that the
Spanish priest administering over his congregation's religious conversion
is speaking English and having it translated into Swahili. She moves on to
the Masai people in East Africa who are known for their nomadic culture
and their large herds of cattle. She goes to Mali to meet the Dogon people
and sits down on one of the pathways to a village and introduces herself
to everyone.[2] She visits marketplaces everywhere and ends up in one in
Cotonou, Benin, where a female seller surprises her by welcoming her by
saying, "So you did come back" (30).

Djanet's mythical journey includes moments of relief and joy but also
moments of frustrations and sadness. Her journey comes to an abrupt stop
when she cannot get into Nigeria because they are changing the currency
and have closed the borders. She decides to stay in a nice hotel in Benin

instead and is suddenly swept back in the world of 1950s France, where songs by Maurice Chevalier serenade the guests and well-dressed businessmen make passes at her. She finally meets her prince, Ben, who was born in Benin but was forced to live in France for much of his childhood, which he disliked intensely because of its inherent racism toward Africans. He sweeps her off her feet and takes her to the ancient palaces at Abomey where he announces that his great-grandfather was the last king there. It is here that her mythical journey receives another jolt. Abomey with all its palaces symbolized the great power Africans held against invaders because the rulers protected their people from the brutality and inhumanity of their invasions. A sense of foreboding overcomes her as she realizes that many of the ancient kings who occupied this palace may have aided the colonialists by procuring slaves for them to be shipped to the new world. Yet, her experience singing with the BaMbuti people in Zaire gives her that eureka moment when she recognizes that they are singing some of the chants and playing the drums from the old Tarzan films.[3] As she sings the Canadian anthem "O, Canada!" using a gospel style, she seems to have found a new identity:

> That's it! See, that's me! The African heartbeat in a Canadian song.
> African Canadian. Not coloured, or Negro . . .
> Maybe not even Black. African Canadian.
> And I close my eyes, and even though I had to have my legs
> protruding from the doorway of the hut, because their huts
> are so small, I began to feel at home. (42)

Saba's journey oscillates between her current predicament of marrying and resettling in Ethiopia and the previous life of her ancestor Sheba, who has decided to meet the great and wise King Solomon. The Canadian Saba is now a director of a company specializing in Ethiopian tours and has not been back to the country since her adolescence. Saba is insecure and uncertain where her future lies, whereas the mythical Sheba is determined and chooses her steps carefully. Fisseha uses her chorus of actors to play contrasting roles in both the ancient and modern scenarios. Tamrin, the commentator and supporter of Sheba in the ancient world, becomes a thorn in Saba's side as a pushy store owner. Ashmodai is the arrogant royal advisor to King Solomon but turns into an intoxicated domestic employee of the modern Solomon. Tamara is Sheba's wise principal advisor but turns into Solomon's opportunist, crafty girlfriend of the present day. Finally, the stern but wise King Solomon turns into Solomon, Saba's softer, fickle boyfriend.

Fisseha draws a sharp contrast between the neat and focused events of the Solomon and Sheba myth and Saba's rather messy modern life. Sheba tells her advisor about her goals for meeting Solomon: "You will lose yourself with me. Let us seek him, Tamara, and we shall find him; let us love him, and he will not withdraw himself from us; let us pursue him and we shall overtake him; let us ask and we shall receive. Let us tame the beast at our door and we shall be at peace" (13). The modern events engulfing Saba, however, appear more like an episode of a soap opera than a long quest for knowledge. Fisseha has turned all of the supporting characters from the ancient myth into self-centered opportunists with human follies. Saba discovers that her future husband is a philanderer and that his belief in following the ancient customs is tenuous. He invites her to the ancient city of Axum, but when she wants to attend an early morning church service, he never wakes up to join her. His hobby is raising doves, and he often compares Saba to one of his creatures. She resents it at first but realizes that it might be a fitting image for her life. She must keep flying just as Sheba did after consummating her relationship with Solomon and then declining his offer for marriage.

Both plays end with moments of first sadness but then satisfaction. Djanet, fueled by the BaMbuti music, rejoices in her "discovery" as she prepares to get on the plane back to Canada. First she sings the following:

> There were times when I felt so insecure
> Never sure
> Where I fit in.
> So I tried to be more like someone else
> But it left me feeling empty inside.
> No matter what people say to me.
> I've got to find my own way to be,
> My own way to be:
> Inside my African heart
> Beats a special part
> That gives me strength, gives me *life.*
> Inside my African soul
> Is where I found the light
> That makes me feel right, makes me whole. (44)

Then she "transforms" herself by pulling out a brilliantly embroidered West African boubou. She puts it on and uses the rest of the fabric to wrap around her head. She is pleased with what she sees.

Saba's last conversation with Solomon sounds like a familiar breakup of two young people, except it contains a spiritual underlining that informs the simple words Saba uses:

> Saba: Do you understand?
> Solomon: You are leaving me.
> Saba: No, I'm simply leaving.
> Solomon: It is someone else.
> Saba: It is somewhere else.
> Solomon: Where?
> Saba: Everywhere.
> Solomon: Take me.
> Saba: I can't.
> Solomon: I will embarrass you with my back-home ways.
> Saba: I am afraid you will lose your back-home ways.
> Solomon: That is no loss.
> Saba: To me it would be the greatest . . .
> Solomon: What am I going to tell my people? They are rehearsing their speeches as we speak. What are you going to tell yours?
> My God, they have not heard from you in months!
> Saba: Not true.
> Solomon: No?
> Saba: I am always home. (60–61)

The journeys Djanet and Saba make certainly fall into the above-mentioned descriptions of diasporic performance methodologies. Both protagonists venture into a mythical world—or at least a mythical consciousness—in order to reframe their identities. This passage leads them not only to discover multiple identities within themselves but to negotiate some of the preconceptions of what modern Africa is. Fisseha creates a clearer connection between mythical and modern Africa by having her actors play roles in both worlds. In effect, she is saying that we all have presences in our mythical histories but sometimes we are unable to negotiate the transformation of these figures into modern life. Djanet's connection is more tenuous. Her attempts at improvising an identity in situations beyond her control seem to only emphasize the frustration of bridging a cultural divide. The men in both women's lives seem ineffectual and unsubstantial. Ben doesn't even appear except as a disembodied voice over the phone. Solomon never seems to reconcile his modern identity with his traditional identity and has no answers for his Canadian wife-to-be. Even the modern "transformations" of the ancient characters have become spiritless and dependent—people who cling to their roles in society and never question them. Perhaps, the modern world does not allow much room for a metaphysical identity and must constantly be reformed in order to establish a connection between current home and former homeland. Diasporic plays such as *Afrika, Solo* and *Wise.Woman* seem to validate what Tompkins wrote: "The construction of identity is always in progress" (39).

NOTES

1. The kingdom of Abomey represents a sacred place. The king has many titles including *Dada* (father of the whole community), *Dokounnon* (holder and distributor of wealth), *Sèmèdo* (master of the world), and *Aïnon* (master of the earth).

2. The Dogon people are strongly oriented toward harmony, which is reflected in many of their rituals. They engage in elaborate rituals when greeting each other, including asking many questions about each other's family.

3. The BaMbuti people are one of the oldest indigenous groups from the Congo area. Known for their hunting and gathering skills, they travel in small groups or bands and are known for their egalitarian nature.

WORKS CITED

Bennett, Zara. "Going Home? The Foiled Myth of Return in Eddy L. Harris' *Native Stranger: A Black American's Journey into the Heart of Africa* and Caryl Phillip's *The Atlantic Sound*." *Paroles gelées* 22.1 (2006): 7–17. Print.

Cohen, Robin. "Diasporas and the Nation-State: From Victims to Challengers." *International Affairs* 72.3 (1996): 507–20. Print.

Dolan, Jill. "Performance, Utopia, and the Utopian Performative." *Theatre Journal* 53.3 (2001): 455–79. Print.

Fisseha, Rebecca. *Wise.Woman*. Unpublished Manuscript. 2009. Print.

Moser, Marlene. "From Performing Wholeness to Providing Choices: Situated Knowledge in *Afrika, Solo* and *Harlem Duet*." *TRiC/RTaC* 29.2 (2008): 239–57. http://www.journals.hil.unb.ca/index.php/TRIC/article/download/18272/1968. Media.

Richards, Sandra L. "What Is to Be Remembered? Tourism to Ghana's Slave Castle-Dungeons." *Theatre Journal* 57.4 (2005): 617–37. Print.

Safran, William. "Diasporas in Modern Societies: Myths of Homeland and Return." *Diaspora* 1.1 (1991): 83–99. Print.

Sears, Djanet. *Afrika, Solo* in *Afrika Solo, Come Good Rain, Je me souviens*. Edited by Ric Knowles. Toronto: Playwrights Canada Press, 2011. Print.

Singh, Shaleen. "Diaspora Literature: A Testimony of Realism." 2008. http://www.EzineArticles.com/1362004. Media.

Tompkins, Joanne. "Infinitely Rehearsing Performance and Identity: *Afrika Solo* and *The Book of Jessica*." *Canadian Theatre Review* 74 (1993): 35–39. Print.

CONCLUSION

Christopher Olsen

The intertextual nature of performance and diaspora studies in the arts and social sciences has generated a lot of attention among scholars across cultures, and, consequently, research in these areas has flourished over the past two decades. Research in dance performance, in particular, has emerged as a fertile ground for comparative studies of performance traditions. However, extensive research on myth performance in dance and drama—especially in their roles in the recuperation and reconstruction of the historical, cultural, social, spiritual, and political realities of African Diaspora communities and especially for African Diaspora people—remains yet to be realized with the same intensity of intellectual study in the academies. Thus, the present study by the three authors in this book seeks to initiate and draw attention to how "performing myth" is applied to artistic and cultural dialogues between African Diaspora communities and their real and/or imagined ancestral origins in a global context.

The essays in this book show the importance of extending diaspora studies to include performance aspects that reflect mythical and spiritual connections and thus not only exposing the shared experiences between these diasporic communities and their ancestral, cultural, historical, and spiritual roots but revealing the cultural connectedness of these dispersed and desperate communities. Because diaspora studies, however, has become such a wide field of inquiry, the scholarship has more often than not tended to expand the perimeters of its definition and classification to include any group of immigrants and their descendants, not only those who were forcibly removed as a group from their homelands and sent into exile, such as took place with the Jewish expulsion from Germany and in the Atlantic slave trade. This overinclusive definition and application of the term "diaspora" is problematic as it generates a lack of consistency in interpretation. The three authors do not make that overgeneralized reading in their essays. To them, African Diaspora peoples mean those of African descent whose ancestors were forcibly removed from the different nations of Africa and enslaved in the Arab world and the Americas during the trans-Saharan and the transatlantic slave trades. The book shows the active desire of African Diaspora communities seeking reconnection with the historical motherland through acts of myth performance in dance and drama in which ancestral African histories, cultures, and identities are reformulated and reconfigured in their new locales, borrowing from cultural retentions. In these acts of myth performance in dance and drama, the authors show that cross-cultural pollination among Diaspora communities with conjured memories of their shared experiences has produced a rich legacy in the performing arts. In particular, these studies have focused on the ability of artists and writers to conjure up a world in which the reader/audience can experience the liminal state around the fault lines that lie between their new world and the old—an area where myth and reality compete for the artists' souls in acts of performance ritual and ritual performance. As Kuwabong discussed in his essay, "Of Rebels, Tricksters, and Supernatural Beings: Toward a Semiotics of Myth Performance in African Caribbean and Afro-Brazilian Dramas," there is a "difference between performance ritual and ritual performance in the context of drama and dance." Whereas performance ritual requires knowledge of "certain laid down sets of rites and/or regulations, . . . ritual performance encapsulates a mythopoeic narrative that conjures up memory" and thus can influence the journey of the Diaspora "pilgrim."

In essence, the book is about a series of journeys made by writers and artists who strive to understand and embody mythical and historical figures from their reconstructed memory of their past in the present Africa. These journeys, both imaginary and real, begin in a reified ancient Africa where contemporary descendants of African Diasporas can locate their own sense of identity through re-visionary historical recontextualization. Sometimes African Diaspora people and their descendants engage mythologies of these certain African deities as their entrée into the life-giving force, known in Yoruba as *asé* or in Bantu language as *nommo* force, to bond them collectively and to create, regenerate, and transform performances and rituals into an ethos of life. As all three authors have ably demonstrated in their reading of dance, some of the journeys begin on the streets and in the dance halls of Philadelphia, whereas others begin in ancient Ethiopia and end on a flight home to Canada. Others begin in Brazil or Cuba and defy the Eurocentric forces that threaten to stifle their voices. The authors have also argued convincingly that some of these mythical journeys circulate seamlessly back and forth between Diaspora communities and their ancestral homes, reinforcing solidarity and shared spirituality. Other journeys are more problematic because the mythicizations are one-sided—the memory constructed turns out to be imaginary, overly romantic, and illusive, and the expectations of the Diaspora pilgrim in relation to the motherland end in disillusion.

No matter the consequences of the Diaspora pilgrim, Africa continues to be a major focus for African Diaspora scholarship and creative journeys into the past. This is underpinned by the universal recognition that the African continent is the birthplace of all humanity and the cradle of human civilization. Some of the world's great civilizations, such as Egypt, Ethiopia, Ghana, Songhai, Zimbabwe, Carthage, Libya, Benin, Kush, Axum, and Mali to name a few, flourished in Africa long before the contact with Muslim Arab and Christian European civilizations and the subsequent colonizations before 1500. When compared to European and Asian societies of the time, in many parts of the continent Africans lived in societies that supported a more democratic governmental system. This perception of ancient Africa continues to attract those who would like to conjure up a nearly utopian vision of that group of societies, considering how difficult it continues to be for modern-day Africans to endure the cultural, physical, psychological, and economic violence perpetrated by the economic greed of global capitalist multinational entities. The attempt to stage this "reality" (in the form of human trafficking) and base it on a mythical story is exactly the journey the artist Lynn Nottage made when she constructed her play *Ruined*.

Finally, in spite of the numerous individual essays written since the 1920s on the links between African worldviews and African Diaspora worldviews in the lives of African Diaspora people, there has not been a gathering of essays together on the theme of myth performance on African drama and dance in the way the three authors here have approached it. Of course, there is the notable exception of Paul Carter

Harrison's definitive 1973 text, *The Drama of Nommo*, which diverged from the approach most books on African Diaspora dance and drama took, which was merely to describe the stage productions and not to include the mythic aspect of performance. This is what this book has strived to rectify; it seeks to begin a debate on the aspects of myth performance toward a more global understanding of African Diaspora performance arts. One of the texts that inspired all of us was *Black Theatre: Ritual Performance in the African Diaspora*, a collection of old essays by different theorists and practitioners of the performance arts of both continental Africans and African Diaspora peoples, edited by Paul Carter Harrison and colleagues. The book, published ten years ago, is a foundational text that examines theatre performance and dance from a theoretical perspective in the context of the African Diasporas. Since its publication, African Diaspora research has broadened its scope to include studies of text and performance among African Diaspora communities all over the globe. For example, plays and dance performances have expanded to reveal how African Caribbean people have rearticulated their "Africanness" within a "Caribbeanness" while re-locating to new communities in the United States, Canada, and Europe. In addition, African Canadian people have found an identity in the historical memories of indigenous Canadian communities. Walcott has been doing this in what is called "meta-theater" or "poetic theater," a performance and dramatic style that incorporates an interdisciplinary approach creating performance pieces out of the African Diaspora "chaos"—using language, dance, music, and strong visual images. Other African Diaspora dramas and performances have worked with similar themes and styles based on scattered cultural memories and mythical journeys, across continents and cultural divides. These are the journeys we scholars and artists must continue to take.

INDEX

ABOUT THE AUTHORS

Dr. Benita Brown is associate professor of dance at Virginia State University. She is the coordinator of the minor in dance within the Department of Health, Physical Education, Recreation, Dance, and Sport Management where she has served since 1999. She is also the founding director of VSU's Sankofa Dance Theatre (1999), a performing arts group that is composed of students that minor in the dance program at Virginia State University. In 2005, she created the dance curriculum at Virginia State University.

Dr. Brown is the recipient of the Choreographer's Fellowship from the Pennsylvania Council of the Arts, the 5-County Arts Fund from Greater Philadelphia Cultural Alliance, the Presenters Stipend from the Virginia Commission of the Arts, and the Virginia's African-American Heritage grant from the Virginia Foundation for Humanities and Social Change.

Her research interests include the study of dance throughout the African Diaspora insofar as the performative studies of spiritual and social dances are concerned. Her recent dance productions include *Black History through Dance*, *A Tribute to Duke Ellington: A Dance Drama*, *Everything's Copasetic: The Bojangles Exhibit*, *Stormy Weather: A Theatrical Dance and Lecture Demonstration*, *The King's Horsemen* (directed by Chris Olsen), and *Private Dancer: A Choreopoem* (Chris Olsen, coproducer). She has studied dance and presented research on dance in Ghana, Gambia, Senegal, Morocco, Bahamas, Jamaica, and Wales and has been published in *African Performatives*, *The Virginia Journal*, *Philadelphia Folklore Project: Works in Progress*, and *Encyclopedia of Women's Folklore and Folklife*.

Dannabang Kuwabong is professor of English at University of Puerto Rico, Rio Piedras Campus, San Juan. He teaches Caribbean and postcolonial literatures. He has researched and published extensively on African Caribbean literature. His research and publications include folklore, gender, and women's issues in Caribbean, African, and African Diaspora literatures. Professor Kuwabong has served as reader for literary competitions organized by the Writers' Union of Canada and University of Georgia Press; he is also an editorial member of the *Journal of Caribbean Studies* and the *Journal of Dagaare Studies*. As a folklorist also, Dr. Kuwabong has published on the culture and literature of the Dagaaba people of Ghana, Burkina Faso, and Côte d'Ivoire. He published *Naa Knga and other Dagaaba Folktales* (1992) and several articles on Dagaaba culture. Some of his work has appeared in *ARIEL: A Review of International Literature in English*, *Journal of the Association for Research on Mothering*, *Canadian Journal of Women's Studies*, *Caribbean Writer*, *Sargasso, Journal of Dagaare Studies*, and *La Torre*, among others. Dr. Kuwabong has three poetry collections to date: *Visions of Venom* (1995), *Echoes from Dusty Rivers* (1999), and *Caribbean Blues & Love's Genealogy* (2008). His fourth collection of poetry, *Voices from Kibuli Country*, is due to be published in the fall of 2013.

Christopher Olsen is associate professor of drama and English at the University of Puerto Rico, Rio Piedras Campus, San Juan. He has written numerous articles on contemporary theater practice with a focus on fringe and experimental theater from the 1960s and 1970s in Europe and the United States. He has also focused on directing and writing about theater in Africa, particularly South Africa. He is the director of a bilingual theater project based at the University of Puerto Rico devoted to presenting freshly translated plays in both Spanish and English and is a long-standing member of Actors' Equity. He is the author of *Off-Off Broadway: The Second Wave, 1968–1980* (2011).